Econocide

Elimination of the Urban Poor

Alice Skirtz

For Michelle
1 Cause you get it!
Alice Skirtz

NASW PRESS
National Association of Social Workers
Washington, DC

Jeane W. Anastas, PhD, LMSW, President
Elizabeth J. Clark, PhD, ACSW, MPH, Executive Director

Cheryl Y. Bradley, *Publisher*
John Cassels, *Project Manager and Staff Editor*
Wayson Jones, *Copyeditor*
Lori J. Holtzinger, *Proofreader and Indexer*

Cover by Naylor Design
Interior design and composition by Electronic Quill
Printed and bound by Sheridan Books, Inc.

© 2012 by the NASW Press

First impression: February 2012

Library of Congress Cataloging-in-Publication Data

Skirtz, Alice
    Econocide: elimination of the urban poor / Alice Skirtz.
      p. cm.
    Includes bibliographical references and index.
    ISBN 978-0-87101-424-5
    1. United States—Social policy—21st century. 2. Public welfare—United States—
History—21st century. 3. Poor—Government policy—United States—History.
4. Poor—Government policy—Ohio—History. 5. Housing policy—United States—
History—21st century. 6. Public housing—Ohio—Cincinnati—History—21st century.
7. Housing policy—Ohio—Cincinnati—History—21st century. I. Title.
    HN59.2.S577 2011
    338.9771'78—dc23

                                                      2011039369

Printed in the United States of America

Table of Contents

About the Author

Alice Skirtz, PhD, MSW, LISW-S, is a long-time member of NASW. She has been active in social work with people who are homeless and economically disadvantaged since the 1960s, is a founding organizer of the Greater Cincinnati Coalition for the Homeless, and continues to be actively involved in local issues of affordable housing and economic equity.

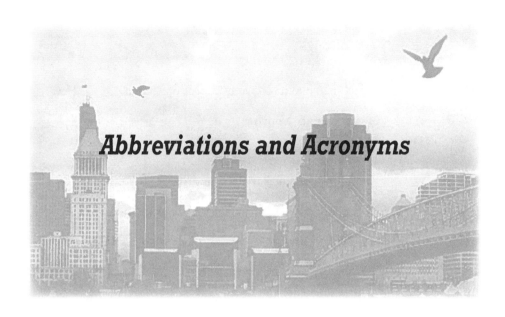

Abbreviations and Acronyms

3CDC	Cincinnati Center City Development Corporation, Inc.
5/3	Fifth Third Bank
AFDC	Aid to Families with Dependent Children
ALI	Anna Louise Inn
AMI	area median income
CBD	Central Business District (Cincinnati, Ohio)
CDBG	community development block grant
CDC	community development corporation
CEO	chief executive officer
CMHA	Cincinnati Metropolitan Housing Authority
CoC	Cincinnati/Hamilton County Continuum of Care, Inc.
CUB	Cincinnati Union Bethel
DCI	Downtown Cincinnati, Inc.
DIC	Drop Inn Center

FICA	Federal Insurance Contributions Act
FMR	fair market rent
GCAEC	Greater Cincinnati Arts and Education Center
HCV	Housing Choice Voucher
HMIS	Homeless Management Information System
HOME	HOME Investment Partnership Program funds
HUD	U.S. Department of Housing and Urban Development
LLC	limited liability corporation
OTR	Over-the-Rhine
PRWORA	Personal Responsibility and Work Opportunity Reconciliation Act of 1996
QHWRA	Quality Housing and Work Responsibility Act of 1998
ReStoc	Race Street Tenant Organization Cooperative
RFP	request for proposals
RLUIPA	Religious Land Use and Incarcerated Persons Act of 2000
SCPA	School for the Creative and Performing Arts
SSC	Social Services Committee (City of Cincinnati)
SSI	Supplemental Security Income
SRO	single room occupancy
TANF	Temporary Assistance for Needy Families
TIF	tax incentive financing
WPA	Work Projects Administration

Introduction

The call came shortly after 3:30 a.m. "Could you come to the emergency room to identify a woman who has died? The only identification she has is your business card tucked in the pocket of her slacks." The caller was a night-shift social worker from our largest hospital—the only trauma center, the hospital obliged to serve indigent patients. Aching from interrupted sleep, but now wide awake, I pulled on a pair of jeans and a warm sweater and drove in the dark night the half mile to the hospital, wondering who this could be. I hoped that the social worker assigned to the dead woman's case would be one of my colleagues with whom I had so often worked getting emergency medical care for the homeless women clients of my agency's shelter, the Emergency Home for Women and Children. Maybe together we could identify the dead woman and, using our social work training, locate her next of kin.

By the time I arrived, a nurse from another department of the hospital had made a preliminary identification. She thought the woman's first name was Sophie—someone who had been in her inpatient unit several weeks earlier for chronic pulmonary problems. The nurse couldn't remember Sophie's last name, making a search for the hospital record nearly impossible, but she thought Sophie had signed herself out "against medical advice" while still quite ill. And, indeed, when the staff pulled the sheet from Sophie's slender body for me to see, I knew immediately it was she, easily identifiable by her reddish-blonde, graying hair twisted under her best floral printed scarf, left askew after the medical team attempted to resuscitate her. She was also identifiable by her hands, with skin hardened and reddened by the chemicals in household cleaning products and years of hard work. There was no doubt, the unidentified woman was my client Sophie, cold, dead on the gurney in the middle of the night, alone, with my card in her pocket her only link to another human being.

Fortunately for me, the social worker on duty *was* one of my colleagues. Together we shifted to that well-practiced place in our social worker heads that protected vulnerable places in our hearts from fully feeling the impact of this early morning moment. My colleague related the details of Sophie's arrival earlier in the evening. The life squad brought her in from a local hotel operated by a compassionate hotelier who provided single room occupancy (SRO) accommodation in shabby but clean rooms for single adults—the furnishings as threadbare as the lives of his clientele. He rented rooms by the day or the week—$13 per day, $69 per week—paid in advance, in cash. Rigid enforcement of the no guests policy kept out the dealers, pimps, and johns—no deals, no tricks—and made the privacy of the tiny hotel rooms safe for single women. In recent years, Sophie had stayed in the hotel intermittently, when she had enough cash earned cleaning houses, also at a daily rate, relieved when she had worked enough days in a row to accumulate $69 for a whole week. In a quiet moment of self-reflection, Sophie told me that she once she needed money so badly that she was driven to "turn a trick," but she was so terrified of the john, who she had found to be really "creepy," that she never tried it again. When she didn't have the money for a room, she would come to the Emergency Home shelter of my agency; if the Emergency Home was full, she would sleep in a local 24-hour self-serve laundry or, sometimes, in warm weather, under the bushes in the park, hoping she could fall asleep unseen, praying that the police would not roust her out of the park, which closed at dusk. But that night, Sophie did not need the few dollars for rent, nor did she have the worry that our shelter would be full or the laundry closed, for she died in the emergency room with her singular connection to another human my name printed on a card. As I was to learn later, her lungs just gave out.

Sophie was 57 when she died, sick enough to be raced to the emergency room by the life squad, but not old and sick enough to qualify for Social Security and Medicare, nor sick enough to qualify for Supplemental Security Income (SSI) or Medicaid for the disabled. I had recently helped her make an appeal of a denial of her application for SSI, based on the dual complications of establishing that her medical condition was severe enough to prevent her from working (after all, she was cleaning houses) and the missing documentation of marriage to her husband. He was a decade older than Sophie but had not been seen for years by anyone, including Sophie. The appeals officer was kind but, closely following all regulations, had ruled that Sophie was able to work and that she was not eligible to apply for Social Security with her husband, who was old enough to have included her as his spouse, if she could find him. Further, she couldn't document that they were ever married, much less that he was still alive. So Sophie continued to work cleaning houses, when she could get the work, and to live between the hotel, the Emergency Home, and the laundry.

That night at the hospital, we phoned Mr. Browne, the hotelier, in desperate hope that his records of Sophie's room rentals might reveal an emergency contact, an old address, or names of others who might know her. He searched old records and found no additional information, just as there was no information on Sophie's current registration, which he had checked earlier in the evening at the behest of the life squad. She did leave a credit balance, as she had paid for the week. Hospital social workers eventually found the name of Sophie's daughter in an old medical record, but as there was no current contact information, the county coroner removed her body to the morgue. Later, the hospital social workers did locate and contact her daughter, who lived in another state. She made arrangements for claiming Sophie's body for burial.

This story of Sophie, like the stories of hundreds of other economically poor people living in urban areas of our most populous cities late in the late 20th and early 21st century, is a largely unseen part of a broader story of economic development, housing policy, and abandonment of civic responsibilities that have forsaken poor people. The location of this story is Cincinnati, Ohio. The story of Sophie's hotelier, Ralph C. Browne (Browne, 1985), supplies another window through which to view the policy-driven legacy of growing economic inequity born of market economies and legislation of contempt for the poor. Several generations of Browne's family were hoteliers, dating back to before the turn of the 20th century, post–Civil War. Specializing in small, residential hotels serving singles, Browne owned several of these affordable hotels in the Central Business District (CBD) of Cincinnati, conveniently located so hotel guests could walk to jobs in restaurants, downtown businesses, or union halls and day labor centers for daily hire. In earlier years, the hotels also served riverboat and railroad workers on overnight layovers from their jobs.

As recently as the 1970s, there were as many as eight or nine of these SRO hotels still in operation in Cincinnati's CBD. Also serving residential needs of single adults were several nonprofit residences for women, the Anna Louise Inn (ALI), the Fontbonne, and the YWCA; for men, there was the Fenwick and the YMCA. All but the ALI have ceased residential hotel operation.

By the late 1970s, Browne's hotels and the nonprofit residences were vulnerable to acquisition and demolition for economic development for public and private projects such as upgrade and expansion of the city's Convention Center, the development of new high-rise hotels and condominiums, and new upscale rental housing. One by one, all of Browne's hotels but two were picked off for economic development, and the nonprofits, save the ALI, were gone, taken for some public, but mostly private, purposes. Those that remained played significant roles in the privatization of the city's economic development to follow. The public discourse at the time focused on expansive development and new construction to make the downtown area vibrant and attractive, and it became clear that the SRO hotels and residences were viewed as standing in the way of progress and as bringing blight and deterioration to the city. Browne was one of few who held a different opinion. In an interview with the *Cincinnati Enquirer*, he found voice to say, "People think of these hotels as flophouses. But there'll always be a need for downtown one-room residences. There are many fine people who live in the one-room houses" (Goodman, 2008, p. B5). Sophie was one of the legions of "many fine people" whose housing options were to be removed and not replaced. These "many fine people" became as disposable as their housing; their presence stood in the way of the market and economic development.

What follows here is an account of how one city used, and continues to use, legislation and administration of public policy for economic development, housing, and privatized management of public assets to dispose of people, mostly poor and perceived as undesirable. Through use of principles of market economy and privatization, the "Sophies" of the community, the "fine people" of Browne's compassionate ethic, and hundreds of others who are economically poor are systematically excluded from the market and placed in jeopardy of removal from the community and from the sphere of civic responsibility.

In this account of a late 20th-century entrepreneurial city, I argue that enactment and implementation of legislation grounded in contempt for the poor, privatization of public decision making, and schemes contrived to keep affordable housing from the market and to reduce or eliminate essential social services result in gross economic inequities. Those largely unseen economic inequities are manifest in a collectivity of poor people I am calling "economic others," those who have the least access to the market economy and to public decision making, who become disposable at the hands of those who have the most access to economic resources and privilege.

In this account, I document ways that, through relentless use of legislative policies and administrative procedures, economic others are repeatedly reputed to be the sole obstacle to economic development, the main cause of reduced property values, and the group solely responsible for downturns in business and that the remedy for such economic problems is seen as removal and disposal of economic others through policies grounded in contempt for their presence in the city. I argue that this is akin to elimination of undesirable populations through unrelenting policy maneuvers, a process I call "econocide"—drawn from the modern word "genocide," which has ancient Greek linguistic origins. In this instance, the *genos* is economic others, the *cide* is destruction or disposal of a collectivity of "undesirables" held in contempt by a larger, economically privileged community. Further, I argue that the disposal of economic others through this process of econocide leaves this population reduced to behaviors found offensive by the economically privileged, behaviors augmented by survival techniques that may compromise economic others' moral standards, making them the object of further contempt.

This work uses the constructs of economic others and econocide to reveal and examine three themes found in relationships of economic inequity occurring across several socioeconomic–political divides during a period of shifts from city government to public–private partnership governance rooted in market-driven goals of economic homogeneity. With a focus on the relationships occurring across socioeconomic divides—accessed through the ebb and flow of actions, affects, and influences from past events along with meanings attached to places and public spaces—this study neither affirms nor excoriates those who promote market economies above all else; nor does it sentimentalize the plight of economic others or vindicate them for using survival techniques that offend the mainstream. The discussions of each of the three themes are informed by factual and affective information and are drawn from perspectives of social justice and civic participation.

The first theme concerns attempts to ensure economic homogeneity by removing economic others from the community through exclusion ordinances perpetrated to remove such individuals from certain places and through development maneuvers, codified by ordinance, that eliminate public and private spaces where groups of economic others congregate.

Unlike the first theme, which examines actual removal of certain people, the second pertains to virtual or indirect removal by policy decisions. It examines ways that local and federal housing policies used to regulate the private housing market and allocate public funds for assisted housing, combined with notions of "deconcentration of poverty," converge to remove economic others by eliminating their housing options from the market. Removal in this instance is of housing, not people, but this results in a contrived scarcity of affordable housing, eliminating economic others from the market and certain communities and neighborhoods.

The final theme traces ways that decisions made through privatization of governance to ensure economic homogeneity absolve the city from responsibilities in social–ethical spheres of obligation to all socioeconomic levels of the city and deny participation in deliberative decision making on public matters to residents at all socioeconomic levels. Privileging private authority over public decision making allows econocide to unfold and actualizes notions of deconcentration of economic others to facilitate their removal.

PART I

Contemporary Economic Inequities and Socioeconomic–Political Responses

Chapter 1

A Collectivity of Economic Others

A collectivity of economic others in the late 20th and early 21st century has recent historical roots in a phenomenon initially described by economist Gunnar Myrdal (1963) as "the underclass." From Myrdal's definition, an economic one describing victims of a postindustrial economy, to the negative meanings added by later social scientists, theorists, and especially journalists, the underclass was soon to become a popular label with evolving pejorative meanings inclusive of ideas of behavior. It came to include descriptors such as "welfare dependency," "intergenerational welfare," and "hardcore American poor," later joined by labels such as deviant, mentally ill or deficient, homeless, homeless mentally ill, and panhandlers. Even Michael Harrington's (1962) widely acclaimed *The Other America: Poverty in the United States* uses a concept of otherness to describe those who are poor in an affluent nation. For Harrington, the poor are unseen and are "other."

In the late 1970s, William Julius Wilson (1980) wrote *The Declining Significance of Race: Blacks and Changing American Institutions*, reframing Myrdal's work, returning to structural economics of deindustrialization and citing its impact on urban ghettos, which led to a class of permanently unemployable blacks, adding the dimension of race to ideas of underclass. The discourse came to embrace Oscar Lewis's (1959) conceptualization of a "culture of poverty" or "enduring poverty," the transmission of poverty from generation to generation in families. Daniel Moynihan (1965) contributed another dynamic to the debate on

the underclass in his work *The Negro Family: The Case for National Action*, joining
the ills of permanent unemployment to behaviors or styles of family formation
that resulted in female-headed households, mostly in the "negro family."

By the 1980s, journalist Ken Auletta (1982) had popularized the term *underclass* for the mainstream press, giving it a pejorative meaning that became code
for describing those who are poor and supposedly responsible for their poverty,
solely due to their own behaviors, not society's economic ills. As noted sociologist
Herbert Gans (1990) writes,

> Auletta's writing established the "underclass" as a behavioral term that lent
> itself to being used as a label beginning with weekly journals of opinion and
> monthly magazines . . . until it diffused into general use in the media over
> the next ten years. (p. 328)

Adding a behavioral dynamic to what had initially been an economic term and
using it as a label to stigmatize and marginalize poor people became an irresistible match for the emerging theories of supply-side economics, growth/market
ideologies, and antigovernment sentiments that heralded the policies of the Reagan administrations and conservative legislatures at both state and federal levels.
Conservative economist George Gilder (1981) and others of the New Right to
follow provided the Reagan administration with theories for domestic and social
policies built on connections between poverty and behavior. In an astonishing
account of marginalization in the area of housing, Gilder (1981) writes,

> As any real estate agent will tell you the three decisive factors in housing
> values are "location, location, location." The chief criterion of a good loca-
> tion, sad to say, is distance from the poor, most particularly from the bro-
> ken welfare families that produce the bulk of America's violent criminals.
> . . . The worth of housing derives from the social values and disciplines of
> a familiar community and access to schools that are not dominated by the
> lower class. (p. 92)

In one brief paragraph, Gilder finds broken welfare families (presumably "broken" relates to marital status of parents) responsible for low property values (not
good location), breeding of criminals (of the violent kind), and diminished social
values (seemingly of the entire community), as they are dominated by the lower
class. His theories continue to describe an economy devoid of distributive justice,
postulating that the best way to reduce poverty is to stimulate the growth/market
economy, "the expansion of demand and income."

Although discourse on the underclass and conservative supply-side economic theories paved the way for politicians to advance policy ideas of welfare reform and transformation of public housing, public discourse pertaining to economic others focused mainly on public assistance provided in federal programs such as Aid to Families with Dependent Children (AFDC) and public housing programs.

Legislation was enacted with companion acts to facilitate "reforms" in public assistance and housing assistance: the Personal Responsibility and Work Opportunity Reconciliation Act of 1996 (PRWORA), generally known as "welfare reform," and the Quality Housing and Work Responsibility Act of 1998 (QHWRA), which came to be popularly called by one of its programmatic names, "Hope VI." Particularized to urban ghettos with black residents, unwed mothers, teenage pregnancies, and deteriorating housing projects, the a racial component of these acts stereotyped welfare and housing assistance as a black problem, even though the numbers of black and white families receiving assistance historically have been about the same (Neubeck & Cazenave, 2001). More specifically, the "underclass" label became synonymous with "welfare queens" and ghetto pathologies of single, unemployed men—mostly black—and drug-infested public housing projects.

At the same time, most American cities were still confounded by the arrival of mentally ill individuals, often destined to become homeless, who had been released from state mental hospitals to life in the community. The Community Mental Health Act of 1964 initiated a decade of deinstitutionalization that was accelerated by the enactment of Title XVI of the Social Security Act of 1935, which provided SSI to disabled individuals. This program—administered by the Social Security Administration, not state welfare departments—provided subsistence income to thousands of mentally disabled individuals who had been "returned to the community." Unlike means-tested eligibility for families receiving AFDC, SSI eligibility was based on documented physical or mental disorders. Many recipients had lived their entire adult lives in institutions and were bewildered by sudden independence. Those who had no family or welcoming community to return to gravitated to urban areas and were disoriented by the ways of big cities. Their vulnerabilities to exploitation, their perceived peculiar behaviors, and their poverty guaranteed them places in the underclass.

For many who returned to the community, even if they had had the capacity to suddenly live outside the institutional setting of the state hospital, SSI was insufficient to cover housing at market rates, food, and ordinary living expenses. Some filled shelters for those who are homeless, others sought cheap housing in SROs. Some resorted to panhandling on the streets of urban areas and the central business districts of major cities for money, cigarettes, or food. Their appearance and behaviors antagonized communities, especially merchants and business owners who did not tolerate panhandling on public sidewalks in front of their establishments.

Several major cities enacted antipanhandling legislation, such as the Seattle, Washington, "Pedestrian Interference Ordinance," which found a person guilty if he or she obstructed pedestrian or vehicular traffic or aggressively begged with the intent to intimidate another person into giving money or goods. (This ordinance was later overturned by *Roulette v. City of Seattle* [1994].) Berkeley, California, amended an existing ordinance titled "Public Peace, Morals, and Welfare" (City of Berkeley, 1994) to include Chapter 13.37, "Limitation of the time, place and manner of solicitation," which forbade behavior that would "cause a reasonable person who was solicited to fear for his or her own safety" and prohibited panhandling after dark. Another, in Cincinnati, titled "Improper Solicitation" (City of Cincinnati, 2010), was enacted to restrict solicitation after dark and in certain locations, such as proximity to automatic teller machines, bus stops, or taxi stands; within six feet of building rights of way or crosswalks; and all public thoroughfares, including sidewalks and streets. This ordinance and companion legislation titled "Improper Solicitation and Sitting and Lying on Public Sidewalks Prohibition" (Cincinnati City Council, 1995b) found popular support, with newspaper headlines screaming "Proposal Gives Boot to Beggars" (Green, 1995) and "Pushing out Panhandlers: Street Beggars Are Driving Away Shoppers and Businesses" (1995).

By the 1980s, the alarmist language and theories of Daniel Moynihan were hailed as prophetic regarding changing dynamics in American "ghettos" (O'Connor, 2001). The right wing of the Republican party began to move national conversation toward welfare reform, severe reduction of government-assisted social services, and profound changes in housing policies that would come to affect economic others in ways unfathomable at the time. Myrdal's term *underclass* no longer had meaning in reference to economic theory but became shorthand for those without economic status, who were marginalized by their poverty, castigated for their behaviors, and rebuked as members of a growing collectivity of economic others.

No more impassioned rebuke of poor people was found than in the Republican party's Representative Newt Gingrich (R-GA), who published and widely marketed his *Contract with America: The Bold Plan by Rep. Newt Gingrich, Rep. Dick Armey, and the House Republicans to Change the Nation* (Gillespie & Shellhas, 1994). With missionary zeal, using his powerful role as Speaker of the House,

Gingrich railed at those poor families who received AFDC for their "dependency," at criminals for making children afraid to go to school on unsafe streets, at the programs of the New Deal, and especially at the War on Poverty. He was particularly harsh toward minor mothers who needed AFDC and those he accused of perpetuating illegitimacy. "Illegitimacy" was never specifically defined in terms of who or what was illegitimate, but the rhetoric included condemnation of teenage pregnancies and births to unwed mothers attributed to the "welfare trap":

> The Great Society has had the unintended consequence of snaring millions of Americans into the welfare trap. Government programs designed to give a helping hand to the neediest of Americans have instead bred illegitimacy, crime, illiteracy, and more poverty. Our *Contract with America* will change this destructive social behavior by requiring welfare recipients to take personal responsibility for the decisions they made. Our *Contract* will achieve what some thirty years of massive welfare spending has not been able to accomplish: reduce illegitimacy, require work, and save taxpayers money. (Gillespie & Shellhas, 1994, p. 65)

A major part of federal legislation that followed the *Contract* was codified narrowly, targeted to reform welfare, particularly PRWORA, ostensibly formulated to change the behaviors of poor people. Unlike the major elements of AFDC, PRWORA sought to improve the economic status of poor families by adding work requirements, time limits on assistance, and admission and/or verification of paternity to establish child support to be paid by parents (mostly fathers) absent from the home, with payments collected by state welfare departments. In addition, the legislation was intended to save taxpayers money, a close cousin to reducing the size of government.

The movement to reform welfare, solidified by the *Contract with America*, included an anticrime component fueled by an emerging "law-and-order" point of view and a spurious, nearly hysterical fear of criminals, especially those committing violent crimes. Gingrich's plan called on government to meet its responsibility to protect streets, schools, and neighborhoods by building more prisons, tightening loopholes that (he claimed) favored criminals, and changing the behaviors of criminals:

> We will cut the "pork" in the recently passed crime bill in order to build real prisons, and we will require criminals to serve their sentences, not have them back on the street to terrorize again and again. And to make criminals more accountable, we will force them to pay full restitution to their victims

or the victims' families. And to those who commit felonies with guns, let us be particularly clear: we will require ten years in jail, minimum, and no exceptions. (Gillespie & Shellhas, 1994, p. 37)

These ideas were introduced in the Taking Back Our Streets Act of 1995, which was never enacted by Congress. However, the threats from criminals—real, perceived, or symbolic—added another group of people to the collectivity of economic others, those returning from prison, who were routinely deemed unemployable and often denied housing, regardless of the severity of their crimes and/ or their having completed their sentences.

Throughout these decades of marginalization of families and individuals for their poverty, economic others of all ages, races, and social or family circumstances struggled to find and pay for housing. Households that benefited from the Fair Housing Act of 1968 and those who economically qualified for public housing faced discrimination, housing shortages, and market-rate housing prices that were beyond their means. Jill Quadagno (1994) describes the legacy of housing policies as steeped in racism and government retreat from commitment to affordable housing:

> Between 1974 and 1983 the supply of affordable housing contracted sharply, while the ratio of rent to income increased significantly. The decline in affordable housing is neither solely nor even primarily a product of random market forces. Rather, it reflects the government's retreat from its commitment to housing the poor . . . for what has made housing support unpopular is its association with efforts to achieve racial integration. This, coupled with the image of public housing as a repository of all the social ills that have triggered white flight to the suburbs, has made subsidized housing the pariah of federal social programs. (pp. 114–115)

Although Quadagno makes a compelling case for the connections between racism and housing discrimination, she writes of those who *have* enough income to qualify for housing assistance, whatever the shortages of units or the peculiarities of housing policy.

Economic others experience the same dynamics of discrimination and housing shortages as those who have a chance at securing housing. Those whose economic poverty makes them eligible for publicly assisted housing are often held in contempt in public discussion. When the waiting list opens for new applications for housing assistance, or when a public project proposes some number of units to be made "affordable" through the program formerly known as Section 8 (from

Section 8 of the United States Housing Act of 1937, also known as the Wagner–Steagall Housing Act), now called Housing Choice Vouchers (HCVs), rhetoric of contempt for the poor escalates. Daytime talk radio excels at inflaming the rhetoric, as it did recently when a proposal was raised that new housing and business development on Cincinnati's riverfront include some affordable rental units, perhaps "Section 8." Radio personality Bill Cunningham regularly broadcasts on WLW 700 AM, inviting his call-in listeners to join him in voicing strong sentiments of contempt on his midday talk show. Said Cunningham (Cunningham, 2008) on the air,

> Section 8 housing dwellers do not live the American dream, they're fat and lazy . . . trashy, living off the tax payers' dole . . . they're fat and flatulent, morbidly obese because they don't have to get up and go to work. . . . If Section 8 moved next to me [melodramatic, sarcastic tone] it's *not goood* . . . [cut to recording of Cincinnati Reds radio announcer Marty Brennaman in a play-by-play account of a baseball game] . . . *"it's not good."* Everyone knows they're fat and flatulent.

Cunningham is not a journalist but an entertainer, so these words provide no information or news, but they do provide a flashpoint for outrage in some sectors of the community for whom he provides public voice. The cruel irony of these contemptible comments, in the instance noted above, is that those who supported HCVs for the riverfront development were those who wanted to prevent or remove HCV recipients from their own communities.

Several recent incidents prompting contempt for HCV recipients took place in open meetings initiated by township trustees to publicly grill officials from the Cincinnati Metropolitan Housing Authority (CMHA) regarding perceived excessive placement of HCV recipients in their townships. The newspaper headline reporting a contentious meeting in suburban Springfield Township, in which Housing Authority representatives were accused of placing Section 8 in the township, read "Leaders Chart Way to Oppose Section 8." The news story begins by saying that "township officials are redoubling their efforts to combat what some residents call the 'gravy train'" and continues with a quote from a township resident: "This program is well intended but it's having consequences that is [sic] lowering property values, affecting school standards and has a very negative crime perception" ("Leaders Chart Way to Oppose Section 8," 2009, p. B1).

In a similar meeting, Colerain Township trustees appeared before the Housing Authority Board, publicly decrying the fact that "the increase in Section 8 housing has contributed to increased crime, more blight and lowered property values in neighborhoods already battered by the foreclosure crisis." The headline for the coverage of that meeting, in 70-point type, reads "Residents Fed Up with Section 8" (2009). That the Housing Authority does not locate landlords for their eligible voucher holders or "place" tenants, with or without the intent of raising crime and lowering property values, seems to be ignored by the trustees and their constituents.

Economic others are excluded as they struggle to acquire enough income stability, eligible family formation, or noncriminal status to qualify for the Public Housing Authority's units or subsidized units with private landlords. Their situation is even more dire in respect to the only other option, market-rate housing, as there is no housing stock in the market at rates they can manage. The situation is especially grave for single people with felony records, who join deinstitutionalized poor mentally ill people in competition for the limited SRO housing found in some poor neighborhoods. Others resort to beds in shelters, and others wander the streets, largely ignored by the market and beyond qualification for any categorical assistance from public resources.

An enduring image understood by most Americans and widely portrayed in the media is that of "the homeless." This label has come to be a pejorative term for those who frequent urban areas, often in retail districts, whose behaviors and appearances are deemed frightening, scary, or abhorrent, stereotyped with the assumption that they do not have a home. Homelessness is a condition sufficiently understood to be described and codified in a federal legislative definition (the Stewart B. McKinney Act of 1987):

> The term "homeless" or "homeless individual or homeless person" includes—
> 1. an individual who lacks a fixed, regular, and adequate nighttime residence; and
> 2. an individual who has a primary nighttime residence that is—
>   A. a supervised publicly or privately operated shelter designed to provide temporary living accommodations (including welfare hotels, congregate shelters, and transitional housing for the mentally ill);
>   B. an institution that provides a temporary residence for individuals intended to be institutionalized; or
>   C. a public or private place not designed for, or ordinarily used as, a regular sleeping accommodation for human beings.

This policy definition pertains to people who regularly or occasionally use temporary shelters as well as to some who eschew shelters at all costs, to the detriment of their health and well-being. This includes those who may frequent parks and public spaces, who sleep in doorways or dumpsters—those places "not designed for or ordinarily used as sleeping accommodation." Less seen in urban areas are those whose transiency and homelessness make them nearly invisible as they frequent one 24-hour retail establishment after another (all-night restaurants, bus terminals, self-serve Laundromats, and so on), sometimes with the approval of attendants or staff, usually not staying long enough to be apprehended for loitering or trespassing.

Along with economic poverty, imputation or ascription of characteristics like deviancy, dependency, or transiency may be a sufficient condition for becoming an economic other; however, policy-driven removal from society's sphere of obligation is a necessary condition. For example, removal of destitute and impoverished people from society's sphere of obligation by elimination of general assistance for singles and "time limitation" of AFDC propels poor adults and families into the collectivity of economic others by means of policy decision.

Provision of a precise definition of economic others is complicated by the amorphous and extraordinary diversity of those who experience poverty, exclusion, and social disposability. Economic others may be single individuals (such as Sophie) or youthful or aging family groups (such as the maligned tenants eligible for HCVs). Like the rest of society, they may be able bodied or disabled; permanently or temporarily housed; male or female; mentally sound or ill; of divergent races, ethnicities, and gender identities; religious believers or nonbelievers; and educated or illiterate. They are as vulnerable to downturns in employment as they are to capricious loss of publicly funded assistance or services to stabilize their economic resources, especially at times of dramatic political shifts in social policies.

As a collectivity, economic others are not a monolithic group easily studied by sociologists or researchers, for they fall into no convenient or simple classifications, nor are they necessarily permanently economic others. The walls of the collectivity are permeable, membership may be transitory or enduring, with people disappearing into the collectivity as they have been removed from the sphere of obligation of the growth/market economy and the government policies attendant to it.

Removal from public spheres of obligation in effect removes economic others from the datasets of public agencies, rendering them "off the information screen" for social researchers and sociologists and invisible to policymakers. They have exhausted public assistance benefits such as Temporary Assistance for Needy Families (TANF), and they receive no Food Stamps or Medicaid; they do not receive public housing assistance, so they are not in welfare or public housing information systems. Although some do appear in the U.S. Department of Housing and Urban Development (HUD) Homeless Management Information System (HMIS) (Cincinnati/Hamilton County Continuum of Care, Inc., 2006), now used by cooperating Continuum of Care shelters and services, the economic others in that system become known only when they enter a shelter or use Continuum of Care services and meet the federal definition of homeless person, as noted earlier.

Because some economic others find employment irregularly or work day labor or seasonal jobs, they and their employers pay withholding and payroll taxes, so they appear in the Federal Insurance Contributions Act (FICA) dataset, where their "otherness" disappears into a broader, usually temporary category of low wage earners. Unless or until they come to the attention of child protective authorities and their children become subject to removal for neglect or abuse, economic other families disappear from welfare datasets. Singles who are economic others usually are unknown to public agents, as most states have had no general relief or general assistance for four decades. Unless or until they come to the attention of the criminal justice system or HMIS on shelter entry, singles, like FICA payers, disappear into the statistics of the larger population.

The disappearance of economic others from datasets and their invisibility to the general public render them not countable or quantifiable and raise question as to where they are. They are often stranded in shelters for the homeless or doubled- or tripled-up with family or friends, as is the case for TANF-exhausted families and families with intermittent qualification for TANF. Single economic others similarly are stranded in shelters, having worn out welcome with friends or family. More frequently, they become transients in urban areas, living on the street or in homeless camps along riverbanks, sheltered by highway overpasses or vacant buildings, or disappearing into public spaces.

Many economic others are unseen, or unseeable, by the general public as their appearance is often indistinguishable from that of everyone else. Unless they are prompted to panhandle for money, hitchhike on public streets or highways, or spend endless daytime hours in public buildings like libraries, bus or train stations, retail stores, parks, or convention centers, they are generally unseen, ignored, and met with indifference or anxious apprehension if encountered "up close." Seen, unseen, or unseeable, economic others are frequently in jeopardy of removal and exclusion.

For the purposes of this study, *economic others* are defined as those men, women, and children who experience intermittent or intractable ravages of economic poverty and rejection—repulsion by mainstream society, placing them in jeopardy of social disposability, especially by removal from spheres of public responsibility. Their disappearance from the public datasets used in policy information systems and research precludes their visibility in public policy decisions. Vulnerable to policy-driven initiatives and maneuvers similar to policies heralding genocide of undesirable populations, economic others face removal from contemporary society by econocide.

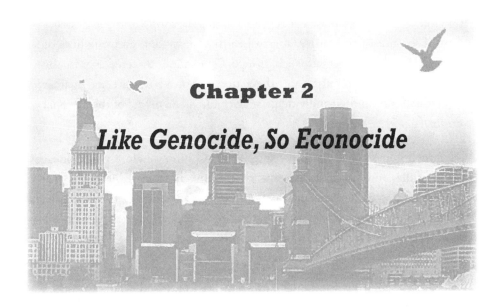

Chapter 2

Like Genocide, So Econocide

The presence of economic others in contemporary society elicits public policy responses from several levels of government, but it confronts current theory and practice pertaining to poverty and "the poor" that are inadequate. Poverty policies based in current poverty knowledge, in narrow, data-driven interpretations of entitlement, dependency, and deviance, result in institutional responses to economic poverty that fail to reach economic others, those who are disregarded by those very institutions. Resulting policy responses tilt toward socioeconomic–political removal of individuals from the community—policies that are reminiscent of policy run-ups to genocide.

The term "genocide" was first constructed by the Polish lawyer and Holocaust survivor Raphael Lemkin (1944) in reference to the mass killings of millions of Armenians, Ukrainians, Jews, Russians, Roma, and Serbs in the 20th century by government perpetrators. Lemkin (1944) coined the new word *genocide* from the ancient Greek word *genos* (race, tribe) and the Latin word *cide* (killing) to mean "the destruction of a nation or of an ethnic group," arguing that it did not mean the destruction of a nation state but, instead, was

> a coordinated plan of different actions aiming at the destruction of essential foundation of the life of national groups, with the aim of annihilating the groups themselves. The objectives of such a plan would be disintegration of the political and social institutions, of culture, language, national feelings,

religion, and the economic existence of national groups, and the destruction of the personal security, liberty, health, dignity, and even the lives of the individuals belonging to such groups. Genocide is directed against the national group as an entity, and the actions involved are directed against individuals, not in their individual capacity, but as members of the national group. (p. 79)

Although Lemkin had studied crimes of mass killings before the Holocaust, his legal studies and scholarship in ethics became his passionate lifework, devoted to understanding of and prosecution of those responsible for the atrocities of Nazi Germany. His work was incorporated into the development of the Geneva Convention on the Prevention and Punishment of the Crime of Genocide.

For Lemkin (1944), genocide has two phases:

one, destruction of the national pattern of the oppressed group, the other, the imposition of the national pattern of the oppressor. This imposition, in turn may be made upon the oppressed population which is allowed to remain, or upon the territory alone, after removal of the population and the colonization of the area by the oppressor's own nationals. (p. 79)

Although Lemkin's work emanated from the horrific events of the Holocaust, he understood victims of genocide to include not only ethnic and religious groups, such as the Jews, but also political and cultural groups. He described and documented genocide as being carried out in political, social, economic, cultural, biological, physical, and moral realms. In the economic realm, foundations of a group's economic existence were crippled to the point of creating "difficulties in fulfilling cultural–spiritual requirements. Furthermore, a daily fight literally for bread and for physical survival . . . deprived [victims] of the elemental means of existence" (Lemkin, 1944, p. 85).

Among the many substantiated genocides in the 20th and early 21st centuries are the well-documented atrocities leading to indictments or actions taken by tribunals or commissions such as the Ottoman Empire against the Armenians (1.2 million victims); the Soviet Union against Ukrainians (>3.1 million victims); Nazi Germany against the Jews, Russians, and Roma (5.5–6.0 million, 3.3 million, and 0.5–1.5 million victims, respectively); Sudan against the Nubians (1.9 million victims); Iraq against the Kurds (100,0000 victims); Bosnia-Herzegovina against non-Serbs (10,000 victims); Rwandan Hutu against the Tutsis (507,000 victims); and Sudan (Darfur) against African tribes (>400,000 victims) (Fein, 2007, Table 6.1, p. 128). These cases and their staggering numbers of victims are representative of genocidal nations and their actions, but only some of those nations have been brought to justice through tribunal or commission action. Roma or Sinti, historically known as "Gypsies," are often included with larger categories of victims of the Nazi "Final Solution," along with victims from other countries such as Poland, Czechoslovakia, Romania, and Russia. Estimates of the number of Gypsies who were victims of the Nazi Holocaust range from 90,000 to more than 1 million (Marglit, 2002).

The inclusion of the genocide of Gypsies in Nazi Germany, although of fewer numbers than the Jews who were exterminated, bears on this study because of the similarities between Gypsies and economic others, as their presence has been subject to national and local laws and policies seeking to control or contain them. Gypsies and economic others may have no primary national identity like the Poles or Ukrainians, but each is perceived as a group with certain cultural patterns and economic existence.

Gilad Margalit describes the two main Gypsy, or *Zigeuner*, groups in Germany—the Roma and the Sinti—and details how they were despised and persecuted by the Nazis for their "otherness." In *Germany and Its Gypsies, A Post-Auschwitz Ordeal*, Margalit (2002) documents German hatred of Gypsies dating back to the 15th century, when Gypsies were stereotyped as thieves, frauds, and parasites living at the expense of "host peoples," who exhibited "wanderlust" but had a romantic side, expressed in music, dancing, or fortunetelling.

In *Bury Me Standing: The Gypsies and Their Journey*, Isabel Fonseca (1995) describes the history of Gypsies in Europe from the 14th century to recent years, a history in which they were feared and reviled as well as romanticized. She portrays Gypsies through stories of individuals and families and illuminates the convoluted saga of how Gypsies and governmental authorities have interacted over time and in several European counties. The transiency and itinerancy of the Gypsies often confounded countries and communities, defying their attempts to regulate and control these "others." One descriptive chapter in Fonseca's extraordinary study is "The Least Obedient People in the World," which reports instances in which Gypsies were "hounded out of town" by authorities; in others, they were "resettled" in attempts by governments to contain them. Writing of contemporary Romanian regimes, Fonseca (1995) cites the brutal regime of Nicolae Ceaușescu, during which "it was somehow imagined that the very existence of the Gypsy minority could be 'solved' by dispersing them among reluctant white communities" (p. 150).

At the beginning of the 21st century, Roma and Sinti populations remain the largest minority in Europe today, estimated to constitute 10–12 million individuals, as reported by Romani Rose (2008), Chairman of the Central Council of German Sinti and Roma. This civil rights organization works with the German government to address ongoing discrimination against Gypsies as well as Jews and is outspoken in its attempts to thwart the efforts of those who deny the Holocaust. Of the marginalization and stereotyping of Gypsies, R. Rose (2008) writes,

> Politically responsible people still deny the existence of racism and discrimination against Roma and Sinti, especially in the countries of central and eastern Europe. Members of the minority are mostly described as a "social problem" and therefore have only themselves to blame for their marginalization and frequently appalling living conditions. Instead of effectively protecting the Roma minorities from discrimination and racism, many politicians contribute to the dissemination of stereotypes and stir up anti-ziganistic, as well as anti-Semitic, feeling in the population. In addition, the media plays an important role in the characterization of racist stereotypes, particularly through the portrayal of criminals as "Roma" or "Sinti," or other such discriminatory terms in press or television reports. (para. 7)

Writing of the 1926 Bavarian *Law for Combating of Gypsies, Travelers, and the Work-shy*, political scientist Guenter Lewy (2000) describes the thinking that went into the law that "imputed a dishonest way of life to all Gypsies," a finding "based more on prejudice than fact" (p. 22) and on itinerant behaviors and stereotyped characterization of Gypsies as criminals. He cites the 1939 draft of a subsequent law that reflected intent to eliminate or control similar groups, including the following (Lewy, 2000, pp.7–9, 202–204):

1. nonsedentary people who could not prove a regular source of income,
2. sedentary individuals who defrayed their living in an illegal manner,
3. the work-shy,
4. people whose way of life endangered the moral life of other members of society,
5. those released from prisons or camps who could not prove a return to orderly life, and
6. minors who had been discharged from institutions because of incorrigibility.

The draft law proposed that such "aliens to the community" be interred in concentration camps. By the time the law was passed, taking effect April 1, 1945, enforcement was limited, as Lewy (2000) writes, "in the interest of the total war effort" (p. 89). Gypsies held in concentration camps were needed for Hitler's army. The types of individuals singled out as aliens to the community were not designated as Gypsies or by race or ethnic heritage but, rather, conditions and behaviors such as not being able to prove regular income, being "work-shy," being released from prison and unable to prove "return to an orderly life," or even aging-out of juvenile institutions. For Lewy, persecution and elimination of the Gypsies by Nazi Germany originated in local and regional policies and practices of authorities to address "social conduct" in decades prior to the rise of Hitler and the persecutions of the Holocaust. The sequential process of elimination began with the idea that behaviors of certain populations were offensive to the mainstream, followed by initiation of laws and procedures for removal and elimination of those populations from society.

Laws like the Bavarian Gypsy Law and related enforcement procedures proved to be complicated for officials of the Nazi party when they came to power in Germany in 1933. Although these laws enabled them to round up and incarcerate Gypsies and other targeted groups, the difficulty was determining exactly who Gypsies were. Just who were the *Zigeuner?* How were they to be distinguished from other citizens? Angus Fraser (1992) reports on the many problems the Reich had in determining the racial purity of citizens and the so-called impurity of those they wished to eliminate. So that they could be distinguished from "pure" citizens, Gypsies as well as the Jews were included as subjects for the Reich's Research Center for Racial Hygiene and Population Biology, housed in the Department of Health. The Center became the locus of testing of Gypsies, but their transiency meant that teams had to locate them in camp sites, internment camps, jails, and eventually death camps. The Research Center was

> the main center for work on the identification and classification of Gypsies and the investigation of links between heredity and criminality: through genealogies, fingerprints and anthropometric measurements . . . to establish a comprehensive tally of everyone carrying Gypsy blood and to determine their degree of racial admixture. (A. Fraser, 1992, p. 258)

Although the Reich met these identifications with a biological and genetic solution wrapped in ideas of race and racial purity, the clarification of who these Gypsies were was expressed in policy and legal definitions complicated by the affect-driven prejudices directed at an itinerate population that was seen as eschewing social convention. Identification of Gypsies, even with the tests and technologies of science, was fraught with problems for the Nazis.

European threats to Gypsies or Roma continue. In the spring of 2008, the Italian government of Silvio Berlusconi, in an attempt to crack down on immigrants, arrested 400 people, holding to Berlusconi's campaign promise to "empty illegal camps and get rid of nomads who have no residence and no means of subsistence" (Rosenthal, 2008, p. A6). In the surge of anti-immigrant sentiment, Gypsies were included. Further, several hundred Italians attacked a Roma camp near Naples with sticks and homemade bombs after a Roma teenager was accused of trying to steal an infant. By July, officials in Rome, working with Italian Red Cross workers, began a census of the Gypsy population, including fingerprinting, that drew criticism from human rights groups and the European Union ("Italy: Census of Gypsies Begins," 2008).

More recently, officials of the European Commission have called out French President Nicolas Sarkozy and the French government for deporting 1,000 Roma in the summer of 2010, likening it to ethnic cleansing, " a situation [we thought] Europe would not have to witness again after the Second World War" (Benhold & Castle, 2010) and stating that is was in violation of European Union law. These deportations were authorized "by a French directive that singled out the Roma as an ethnic group," with Sarkozy referring to the Roma camps as a "source of crime and prostitution" (Benhold & Castle, 2010).

Throughout these several accounts of Gypsies, themes of imagining and marginalizing Gypsies as "others" and then "solving" the Gypsy problem by national or regional public policy or legislation endure. Implementation of the policies has required actions ranging from relatively benign—exertion of sufficient social pressures to drive Gypsies out of town—to horrendous—extermination of nearly 1 million Gypsies in Nazi death camps.

"Aliens to the community," "the work-shy," "nonsedentary people who cannot prove a regular source of income," "parasites living at the expense of 'host peoples'," "nomads with no residence and no means of subsistence"—these terms and phrases have a striking similarity to those used in accounts of contemporary urban conditions originating in economic inequities. "Underclass," "panhandlers," "beggars," "deadbeat dads" and "welfare moms," "the mentally ill," and terms used pejoratively like "*the* homeless," "street people," "fat, flatulent Section 8," and even "Section 8" used as code for victims of housing discrimination, resonate with those terms of earlier times and other places emanating from the hatred that spawned genocide.

Economic others face social and political restrictions and impediments to their situations similar to those faced by Gypsies and Jews and others in the genocides of historical and more recent times. Although not representative of a particular race or an ethnic group like the Roma, or a culture like that of the Jews of the Holocaust, the collectivity of economic others of contemporary times exists in similar jeopardy of social and political elimination through use of public polices driven by market economies—social and political policy-driven econocide.

Documented histories of genocidal atrocities and the policy developments preceding genocide, as well as established theories pertaining to genocide, provide a context for this study of the contemporary phenomenon of econocide. Only a few authors have used the term "econocide," notably Seymour Drescher (1977), who in *Econocide: British Slavery in the Era of Abolition* uses the term to shed light on the destruction of a British economy that was decreasingly dependent on slavery as a result of market declines, coincident with emerging British abolitionist ideas.

A more recent use of the term is found in the work of Arjun Appadurai (2006), who speaks to the ethical sequelae of market economies and globalization on urban communities worldwide as well as related losses of and failed development of employment opportunities. He raises questions of winners and losers in globalization:

> Are we in the midst of a vast worldwide Malthusian correction, which works through the idioms of minoritization and ethnicazation but is functionally geared to preparing the world for the winners of globalization, minus the inconvenient noise of its losers? Is this a vast form of what we may call econocide, a worldwide tendency (no more perfect in its workings than the market) to arrange the disappearance of the losers in the great drama of globalization? (Appadurai, 2006, p. 41)

Disappearance of the losers who are excluded from "the great drama of globalization" would come to include the disappearance of economic others who cannot participate in growth/market economies of the world or their own local communities.

Sociologist Helen Fein (2007), director of the Institute for the Study of Genocide, provides working constructs for the study of genocide, terror, and slavery that are relevant to this study in her descriptions of the preconditions of genocide and issues required for each of those phenomena to be manifest. For the emergence of genocide, she includes the following elements (Fein, 2007, p. 19)

+ There is solidarity/exclusion of victims from the universe of obligation,
+ the victims constitute a group,
+ there is conflict at times over the legitimacy of the victims' group,
+ there is real threat from the victims' group, and
+ there is perceived or symbolic threat from the victims' group.

This understanding informs and provides ways to understand the precarious position of those who are poor and become economic others in contemporary market economies. Notions that poor people pose "perceived or symbolic" threats to a larger, more privileged community set the stage for their exclusion from the universe of obligation. Paralleling Fein's understanding of genocide, the victims in the case of econocide are affiliated as a group defined or unified by their economic poverty, their "economic otherness," and by their marginalization and exclusion from mainstream society.

Contemporary relationships and public policies pertaining to economic others and econocide described in the following pages have been referenced by some as manifestations of "gentrification" or "ethnic cleansing." The examples do have some similarities to recent interpretations of ethnic cleansing that, like genocide, have elements of removal of unwanted groups. The United Nations definition of genocide is "the deliberate and systematic destruction of a racial, political or cultural group," and its definition of ethnic cleansing is "the elimination of an unwanted group from a society, as by genocide or forced migration" (Becker, 1995). The United Nations and Geneva Conventions accept Lemkin's definition of genocide as a crime against humanity, in times of peace as well as war.

For many scholars, the broader definition of ethnic cleansing encompasses both genocide and massed killings. Alain Destexhe (1995), Secretary General of Doctors Without Borders, writing of genocide in Rwanda, argues that there have been only three instances of genocide in the 20th century: Armenians killed by Turks; extermination of Jews, Gypsies, and homosexuals during World War II; and slaughter of the Tutsis by the Hutus in Rwanda (Destexhe, 1995; see also Becker, 1995). As envisioned here, econocide has a meaning closer to crimes against humanity and to Destexhe's understanding of World War II genocide against groups of Gypsies and homosexuals than it does to broader ideas of ethnic cleansing.

Drawing on an understanding of genocide as arising from relationships between victims perceived as constituting a group and perpetrators seeking to exclude those victims from society's universe of obligation, this study demands more than sociological description or historical documentation. It requires inquiry into the dynamics of those relationships across socioeconomic–political divides and inequities in which some—economic others—become invisible, and others—members of a powerful mainstream —orchestrate their disappearance by policy decisions rather than forced removal or mass killing. These dynamics confound and defy common understanding due to the elusiveness of both the powerful and the others—the powerful for their callous, relentless use of bureaucratic, policy-driven maneuvers to eliminate economic others, and the others for their inability to resist such maneuvers and their use of survival techniques that eschew social conventions, often risking compromise of their moral standards.

PART II

The City and Econocide: Cincinnati, Ohio, and Policy-driven Elimination of Economic Others

Recent history of social and political dynamics of the city of Cincinnati provides a contemporary example of social and political precedents to econocide through removal of economic others from the community. Offered here as a narrative drawn from the perspective of civic experience and participation are profiles of policy actions—antipanhandling, drug exclusion, relocation of transitional housing programs, and use of public areas—aimed at direct removal of some people from certain neighborhoods to benefit business and preferred socioeconomic purposes, policies that also result in the removal of economic others from the sphere public obligation.

The descriptions of policy-driven actions here reveal a set of circumstances akin to the preconditions for genocide described by Fein (2007): The victims constitute a group, there is conflict over the legitimacy of the victims' group, there is real threat from the victims' group, and there is perceived or symbolic threat from the victims' group. The victims include both law-abiding economic others who use public spaces by day and/or transitional housing by night as well those who engage in miscreant behaviors, such as loitering and drug use.

For many targeted by the policies described here, the socioeconomic origins of many of their behaviors and daily habits are found in market-driven housing policies that have eliminated affordable housing options. Having been closed out of housing, economic others turned to shelters, social services, or the streets for survival. Like those of many major cities, Cincinnati shelters remain fully utilized; in 2009, 8,525 homeless people (unduplicated count of men, women, and children) used emergency shelter, street outreach, and transitional supportive housing services (Cincinnati/Hamilton County Continuum of Care, Inc., 2010a). That number does not include those who experienced homelessness surviving on the street or in homeless camps at the river or beneath highway underpasses but did not use homeless services and, hence, were never registered in the HMIS database. They became targets, not just for removal from streets and neighborhoods, but also for exclusion from the sphere of public obligation.

In 2009, the CMHA reported a waiting list for families eligible for HCVs rising to nearly 10,000 and nearly full occupancy in CMHA-owned subsidized units (Affordable Housing Advocates, 2010a). The waiting list had been closed for three years. Affordable Housing Advocates (2010b) report a loss of 2,000 affordable housing units between 2000 and 2010.

Although this study describes the dynamics and experiences of one city, it is probably representative of similar sociopolitical–cultural dynamics in other large entrepreneurial cities where similar conditions and relationships of economic inequity exist. The example of Cincinnati is documented by legislative initiatives of municipal government; by newly established privatization of functions previously held by government; and by initiation and implementation of administrative policy decisions related to housing, economic development, planning, delivery of social services, and management of public assets and spaces.

Many of the ordinances and resolutions of city governance described here, especially those pertaining to housing policies and planning, were adopted citywide. Some pertain to specific geographical districts—for example, the CBD (downtown) and certain neighborhoods. Two of the city's 52 statistically and geographically identified neighborhoods are repeatedly singled out as sites for removal of economic others, their housing options, and their providers of social services. These two neighborhoods are known as Over-the-Rhine (OTR) and the West End, adjacent communities sharing geographical boundaries with the CBD, once known as the Basin. Both areas are sought for private development of upscale housing, mostly restricted to home ownership, and to arts-related development, such as relocation of the Art Academy (a private college), new construction to relocate the School for the Creative and Performing Arts (a public K–12 school), and privately owned boutiques and small "artsy" businesses.

Both OTR and the West End are among Cincinnati's oldest neighborhoods, each home to its poorest residents and oldest housing stock. The iconic name Over-the-Rhine is an ethnic label/epithet dating back to the mid-1800s, when German immigrants populated the neighborhood on the "other side" of the

Miami Erie Canal. Instead of "Germantown," as it might have been named, it became known as the neighborhood reached by going over the Canal, or "over the Rhine." The West End is the home of the first public housing projects built after the New Deal for slum clearance/blight removal under provisions of the newly organized CMHA. The first buildings were racially segregated, with white tenants in Laurel Homes and black tenants in Lincoln Court. Although most of the original buildings are now gone, demolished as a result of Hope VI redevelopment of public housing projects in favor of "mixed-income communities," the scars of segregation remain.

Both OTR and the West End are home to the city's oldest and newest social service agencies serving economic others—some have been in continuous operation for more than a century (Cincinnati Union Bethel [CUB], since 1830; The Salvation Army, since 1890; Santa Maria, since 1897). Many were founded by religious organizations, with shelters for homeless singles and families; soup kitchens for the hungry; protective day services for young children and elderly; transitional and permanent supportive housing for those in recovery from addiction or mental illness and intractable economic poverty; and, until recently, an abundance of federally subsidized rental housing. As the following descriptions reveal, that abundance has nearly disappeared, leaving a contrived scarcity of affordable housing in the market and few units with subsidies. Similarly, attempts at removal or relocation of essential social services reflect another step in removing economic others by econocide.

Just as the pre-Holocaust 1926 Bavarian Law is seen as an attempt to remove Gypsies and other undesirable populations from an envisioned racially homogenous society, this study describes relentless attempts to remove economic others from an envisioned economic homogeneity through a contemporary phenomenon I name econocide. In chronological order, the legislative and administrative policies and decisions related to direct removal of economic others—individuals as members of a group to be eliminated or removed from the community—considered here are these:

+ Panhandler Ordinances (1995);
+ incorporation of Downtown Cincinnati, Inc. (DCI) (1995);
+ Drug-Exclusion Ordinance (No. 229-1996) to exclude those arrested for illegal drug abuse and/or related crimes from OTR (1996);
+ organization of the Greater Cincinnati Arts and Education Center (GCAEC) to relocate the School for Creative and Performing Arts (1996); and
+ redevelopment of Washington Park (2009).

The initiatives, resolutions, ordinances, and policy decisions considered here have overlapping time frames and social–cultural interconnections. Considered alone, each may be seen as having merit at a particular point in time and/or for minority interests. However, the totality of the repeated attempts to remove economic others whose presence or behaviors are deemed undesirable, alongside relentless undermining of affordable housing options and surrendering of public planning and housing decision making to private interests, followed by attempts to restrict geographical locations of social services for economic others, extended over time, establishes a policy framework for systematic removal of economic others akin to genocide. Using policies of market economy augmented by contempt for those who have the least access to the market, such genocide-like tactics becomes a legal crime of econocide—a collectivity of victims disappears, removed from the market *and* thereby the community, sanctioned by a collectivity of the privileged with a goal of economic homogeneity.

Chapter 3

Beggars, Panhandlers, and Public Policy

Hark, hark! The dogs do bark,
The beggars are coming to town,
Some in rags, some in tags,
And one in a velvet gown.

—Mother Goose

. . . princes, lords, and counselors of state, and everybody should be prudent and cautious in dealing with beggars. . . . These are beggars who have neither the signs of the saints about them, nor other good qualities, but they come plain and simply to people and ask an alms for God's, or the Holy Virgin's sake: —perchance honest paupers with young children, who are known in the town or village wherein they beg, and who would, I doubt not, leave off begging if they could only thrive by their handicraft or other honest means, for there is many a godly man who begs unwillingly, and feels ashamed before those who knew him formerly when he was better off, and before he was compelled to beg.

—Martin Luther, *Liber Vagatorum*

I, however, am a bestower: willingly do I bestow as friend to friends. Strangers, however, and the poor, may pluck for themselves the fruit from my tree:

thus doth it cause less shame. Beggars, however, one should entirely do away with! Verily, it annoyeth one to give unto them, and it annoyeth one not to give unto them.

—Friedrich Nietzsche, *Thus Spake Zarathustra*

Throughout history, societies have struggled with the presence of beggars—how to regard them, how to give to or rebuke them, even how to regulate them. Whether announced by barking dogs, as in the Mother Goose rhyme; viewed as unwilling to beg if they could thrive by the other "honest means" of Martin Luther's account; or seen as something to be done away with, avoiding the annoyance of giving or not giving, referenced in Neitzsche's *Zarathustra*, the presence of beggars is confounding. In contemporary urban society, beggars are named panhandlers, and their behaviors of stopping others on the street or in public spaces to ask for money or food are perceived as disconcerting and are subject to regulation by public policy. Differences between the verbs *to beg* and *to panhandle* have been clarified for contemporary use and for use here in *Clark et al. vs. City of Cincinnati* (1995, 1998), which states that "begging is to ask for as a charity" and "panhandling is to accost [people] on the street and beg from [them]." The court's clarification uses the term "solicit" to encompass both begging and panhandling. In many ways, contemporary urban panhandlers are viewed as the Gypsies were in the 1926 Bavarian Law: as nonsedentary people who cannot prove a regular source of income or, when subjected to laws to regulate them, as sedentary individuals who defray their living in an illegal manner, even as "work-shy."

This account of a series of ordinances to regulate panhandlers enacted by the city of Cincinnati is a contemporary example of attempts through city governance to remove and dispose of panhandlers precipitated by downtown business interests. It begins in 1995 with ordinances proposed to change the section of the Municipal Code popularly called "Aggressive Panhandling" to forbid panhandling or begging in downtown and neighborhood business districts. These legislative maneuvers were aggressively promoted by the newly formed development district DCI, but they failed as courts repeatedly ruled that panhandlers have a right to free speech, which includes panhandling or begging. There had been previous failed attempts to license panhandlers, similar to the permits issued to street vendors. In 2002 and 2003, attempts were again made to forbid panhandling, again failing. Although they were not able to ban panhandling outright, the 1995 modifications of the "Aggressive Panhandling Ordinance" described here succeed partially, permitting only silent or passive panhandling, as the following account shows. The main theme of this account is focused on the social and legislative dynamics of the two ordinances that changed "Aggressive Panhandling" to "Improper Solicitation."

If this 1995 saga of private initiative directed at public policy to eliminate a perceived social problem were portrayed as theater, the narrative drama might read as follows:

Begging the Question

(An urban narrative drama in three acts, enlightened by Mother Goose, Martin Luther, and Friedrich Nietzsche)

Characters

Barking Dogs	Downtown Cincinnati, Inc. (DCI)
	Business and Retail Interests
	Downtown Residents Council
Princes, Lords, and Counselors of State	Members of City Council
	U.S. District Court
Beggars	Panhandlers,
	economic others

Townspeople, housed and homeless residents, voters, visitors

Place: Cincinnati, Ohio

Time: Circa 1990s

City Population: 350,000 in a metropolitan area of 2.1 million

Governance: Home rule by charter, with a nine-member city council elected at large

Synopsis: This story has its beginnings in antiquity, immortalized in the timeless drama of contempt for beggars. The context of this chapter of those ageless stories lies in privatization and economic inequity, wherein business interests prevail in persuading legislators to adopt policies to drive beggars from the public square. In the end, beggars prevail as the court protects their rights of freedom of speech and due process but restricts begging to passive behavior carried out in silence. Beggars are driven deeper into the collectivity of economic others while business interests are frustrated in their attempts at removal.

Act I

"Panhandling prevents many visitors from experiencing and enjoying our beautiful downtown," wrote David C. Phillips (1995, p. A11), then CEO of DCI. He went on to say that "when we meet with retailers and building owners, we hear repeatedly that panhandling adversely affects downtown businesses and others by driving customers away and feeding the perception that our downtown is unsafe" (Phillips, 1995, p. A11). These statements were published in an op-ed in the *Cincinnati Enquirer* under the sardonic headline "Begging the Question" (borrowed here). Phillips's editorial is subtitled "Downtown's Future Depends on Stopping Panhandling."

Published in the same op-ed location was an opposing view written by Pat Clifford (1995), then Coordinator of the Greater Cincinnati Coalition for the Homeless, under the title "DCI's Mean-spirited Crackdown Would Be Ineffective." Clifford (1995) cites information from DCI's recently published study that "panhandling is the least of downtown's problems. Parking availability and evening/weekend hours were the number one shortfalls" (p. A11); he goes on to say that "the crackdown will be ineffective because arresting people will not stop panhandling or poverty. Believing it will, however, is causing jail cells to replace social services in local, state and national budgets" (p. A11).

The communitywide discourse reflected in the Phillips and Clifford editorial pieces followed the City Council's consideration of councilmember Phil Heimlich's proposed "Panhandler Ordinance," introduced at the unrelenting request of DCI, downtown business and real estate interests, and the Downtown Residents Council. The intent was to amend the "Aggressive Panhandling" section of the Municipal Code with two ordinances to outlaw panhandling. The first ordinance proposed a section titled "Sitting and Lying on Public Sidewalks," prohibiting the same by Ordinance No.155-1995; the second, Ordinance No.156-1995, added "Improper Solicitation" as a means to "regulate and prohibit solicitations which affect the public safety of citizens using the public sidewalks and streets."

Public discussion of these ordinances included consideration of proposals made by DCI to provide services to panhandlers, initially with a proposal to seek donations from customers of local merchants to provide "Real Change, not Spare Change" to agencies like The Salvation Army to use to care for panhandlers (a failed program tried in other communities). That proposal for service was later modified to provide outreach services to panhandlers, supposedly to dissuade them from begging (a modified version of this idea was later initiated by DCI). Public discourse on Heimlich's proposed ordinances followed, mostly by those with passionately held opinions—"Give beggars the boot!" and "No panhandling"—and a minority response from councilmember Bobbie Sterne (Greene, 1995): "It's nonsense and its provisions Draconian" (p. A1). Heimlich (1995) publicly revealed his position: "To be honest, what I am trying to do is make panhandling illegal. The courts will not permit that so I have built the strongest ordinance possible that I think the court will allow" (p. 7).

At the time of this discourse, using the available section of the Code for "Aggressive Panhandling," few arrests had been made. During the 12 months of April, 1994 through March, 1995, 23 citations had been issued to 19 different individuals (Cincinnati Police Department, 1995). Two of the arrests were made in outlying areas, not downtown—one was of a juvenile, and one was cited as having occurred at the police headquarters address. However, 15 of the arrests were made during six weeks of Christmas holiday season, in the downtown Fountain Square area during what the police department called the "Christmas crackdown," an annual, well publicized effort to prevent seasonal shoplifting and, in 1994, panhandling. The citations are fourth-degree misdemeanors.

Act II

Two ordinances, No. 155-1995 (Cincinnati City Council, 1995a) and No. 156-1995 (Cincinnati City Council, 1995b) were passed by the City Council on May 3, 1995, the former modifying the Code regarding sitting or lying on public sidewalks to prohibit interference with pedestrian traffic in areas designated for commerce, the latter regulating improper solicitation by place, times of day, and activity defined as "solicitation" (asking for money or goods, whether by words, bodily gestures, signs, or other means of communication). The ordinances were enacted for a period of six months as a trial to be reconsidered by Council. Immediately after adoption, several court challenges resulted in rulings that forbidding panhandling violates First Amendment rights of free speech, that the ordinances be required to provide due process, and that the "lying on the sidewalk" section had to be excluded (it is covered elsewhere in the Code). The Municipal Code (City of Cincinnati, 2010) was modified to incorporate the two ordinances. By 2001, the content of the ordinances proposed in 1995 had been adopted by the Council, combined in section 910-12 of the Code, "Improper Solicitation," now used by the police department to cite panhandlers with a fourth-degree misdemeanor for a single offense and a third-degree misdemeanor for three or more violations within one year.

Act III

Section 910-12 regulates panhandling by place and time of day and through prohibition of behavior such as use of profane language and gestures and making
false claims such as misrepresenting one's poverty or military service. Although
the intent of this legislation was to forbid panhandling, ostensibly to save downtown business, arresting and removing panhandlers from the downtown retail
and entertainment area, it accomplished this goal only in part due to the codifica-
tion of solicitation. Section 910-12 defines solicitation as making any request in
person in a public place for money or goods when the requestor does not know
the respondent. The definition continues:

> However, the terms "solicit" and "solicitation" shall not mean the act of pas-
> sively standing or sitting with a sign or other indicator that a donation of
> money, goods or any other form of gratuity is being sought without any
> vocal request other than a response to an inquiry by another person.

As the Code now stipulates, panhandling is legal if pursued within the proper
hours of the day and parameters of space and proximity to buildings and streets,
by those who may sit or stand silently and may hold signs indicating a gratuity is
sought from someone not known to the sign holder.

Measurement of the impact of the panhandler ordinances and the resulting
legislation is not possible by comparison of arrests and citations from previous years, as the Code has been changed. However, in the annual Quality of
Life Index reports made by the city manager to the City Council, statistics are
included on panhandling citations citywide. In the years 2004–2008, citations
in the range of 140–200 annually were reported—two to four per week on average, hardly the major influence on deteriorating retail sales trumpeted by DCI
and the downtown business interests who forced the legislation. Panhandlers are
visible on downtown streets; in public spaces such as grassy areas at highway exit
ramps; and sitting or standing next to retail establishments at the proper distance from ATMs and banks, bus stops, and taxi stands and on pedestrian walk-
ways to sports venues all within the prescribed hours of 7 a.m.–7 p.m. (7 a.m.–8
p.m. during daylight saving time). Because they may not speak to ask for money
or gratuities, most panhandlers hold hand-lettered cardboard signs: "Hungry,
please help," "Help the Homeless, God Bless You," "Homeless Vet Need Food,"
"Hungry and Homeless." One sign recently boldly stated, "I'll be honest, need
money for beer."

Epilogue

The matter of panhandling in the city of Cincinnati has been "settled" by the courts, or not. Two episodes have resurrected panhandling years after the courts determined it to be legal, and the Municipal Code was amended accordingly. In 2002, then-mayor Charlie Luken raised panhandling again when the GCAEC was deliberating about a new site in OTR for the School for Creative and Performing Arts. Of the proposed sites, all were in proximity to Washington Park, the city's six-acre urban public park, and the Drop Inn Center (DIC), the City's largest shelter for single men and women, located diagonally across from each other at the intersection of 12th and Elm Streets. Daily use of the park by several dozen adults, reputed to be homeless, panhandlers, *and* DIC clients became a flashpoint for the narrative surrounding site selection for the school, vicariously providing "cover" for those who wanted to remove the DIC.

Day use of the public space in Washington Park has a rich history. Formerly a Presbyterian cemetery and converted to a park in 1855, it was described in the *WPA Guide to Cincinnati 1788–1943* (Works Progress Administration, 1943/1987) as having "a ball diamond, swimming pools, horseshoe pits, and an old fashioned bandstand [still there in 2010]. On warm sunny days in the park, benches are filled with people who loaf and invite their souls" (p. 221). In contemporary vernacular, such use might be described as "chillin" or "hangin' out in the 'hood"—rather like the "loafing and inviting [one's] soul" of an earlier time. No doubt some of the day users chillin' in the park also use the DIC, as the center has served up to 450 homeless adults each day with overnight shelter, food, and social services in the same location for nearly three decades, across the street from the 147-year-old park. As the plans for locating the school near Washington Park were discussed, Mayor Luken publicly and repeatedly asserted that the frequent users of Washington Park were criminals, deviants, homeless, panhandlers, and somehow affiliated with the DIC.

Although there was scant evidence that Luken's description of users of the park was accurate, his statements resonated with the public, and pressure began to build, not to locate the school at another site but to remove the DIC in the name of eliminating panhandling. "Mayor Puts Pressure on Shelter" reads the *Enquirer* headline for a story that describes the DIC as the "latest combatant in the city's war against panhandling" and relating how "Mayor Charlie Luken is insisting that the homeless shelter denounce panhandling by its residents and refuse services to people who commit crimes" (Korte, 2002b, p. B1). Eventually the school was built at the corner shared with the park and DIC; however, this episode introduced spurious connections between panhandling and social services, attempting to legitimize de facto punishment for the legal behavior of panhandling by denial of shelter services for the sake of removing some people from the park.

Although no policy changes were made by either the city (panhandling is legal) or DIC (panhandling is not a criterion for shelter admission or discharge) in the matter of Washington Park and the school, the commingling of shelter admission and panhandling was to emerge again in 2010. This time, the context shifted to city funding for shelters for the homeless and the standards used for qualifying shelters. Shelter providers had collaborated in self-regulation using standards developed and implemented together with the city more than 20 years earlier and updated as recently as 2009. The codified (and approved by the city) *Minimum Standards for Shelters* was developed to address such matters as safety (building, fire, health); zoning and occupancy as permitted by the city; fiscal solvency and audits; adequacy of services, such as staff:client ratios; social service practices; client confidentiality; and record-keeping. Shelters were certified as meeting the standards by a peer-review system managed by the Greater Cincinnati Coalition for the Homeless. The Coalition is not a provider of services for the homeless but is an advocacy group of member providers of services for those who are homeless. It exists in a culture of consensus-building and program neutrality, not favoring one service or program over another.

The Coalition developed working peer-review teams to certify shelters as meeting the standards; the city accepted the certifications as one criterion for funding. Teams included city fire, health, and building department officials (who could issue citations for violations of city codes) along with other shelter providers, facilitating meaningful shelter reviews; tough-minded peers and city officials could deny certification and assist with making corrections to bring programs in compliance with the standards. Certification that shelters meet the *Minimum Standards* is one criterion for city funding.

In 2010, the City Council resurrected the notion that panhandling needed to be eradicated, once again making the spurious connection between panhandling and homelessness in the ideological leap *panhandler = homeless = shelter client*. Although panhandling had been found legal by the courts and could not be forbidden by the city, antipanhandling notions could be codified in requirements for shelter funding. The Council added a new standard to the *Minimum Standards* that required shelters to "develop policies to discourage panhandling, and to develop clear and consistent consequences to be enforced if a shelter client is known to panhandle" (Cincinnati City Council, 2010a, 2010b). With this revision, the *Minimum Standards* were to be retitled *Shelter Program, Operations, and Facility Standards.*

To ensure that shelters would be certified under these new standards, the City Council removed the certification process from the Greater Cincinnati Coalition for the Homeless, handing it off to the Cincinnati/Hamilton County Continuum of Care, Inc. (CoC), the public–private partnership newly responsible for all planning and funding decisions for public funds for homeless service programs. This policy shift inaugurated a gross conflict of interest: The privatized entity charged with allocating all public funds for shelters also certifies shelters for funding, jeopardizing accountability of both funding decisions and certification. It is like having public budget and expense reports or corporate tax returns prepared and audited by the same entity. The Greater Cincinnati Coalition for the Homeless, a single homeless man who legally panhandles, and one shelter have joined together to file a complaint in federal court against the city, seeking removal of the "panhandling" standard from the *Minimum Standards* and relief from the restrictions on protections by the First Amendment to panhandle (*Eggleston, Greater Cincinnati Coalition for the Homeless, Grace Place Catholic Worker House v. City of Cincinnati*, 2010).

One irony of this entire episode is the enormity of the policy in proportion to the problem of panhandling. Those who advanced the insertion of the "antipanhandling" standard generally locate the problem in the vicinity of the DIC shelter in OTR and in the downtown CBD. As reported by the *Cincinnati Enquirer,* under headline "Panhandlers in Spotlight Again" (Krantz, 2010), there are only a few people known to panhandle—"police and outreach workers know 16 people at most in the downtown area" (p. B1).

The timelessness of this drama around begging—revealed in the behaviors of economic others, business interests, and public policymakers—provides a glimpse of this problem in one major American city. Considered alone at a particular point in time, these episodes may be of some interest to sociologists, social activists, politicians who deal with urban problems, city administrators, and scholars of the First Amendment. However, they provide a beginning reference point for a larger narrative of changes in an entrepreneurial city with growing gaps in economic equity and growing influences of business interests and privatization.

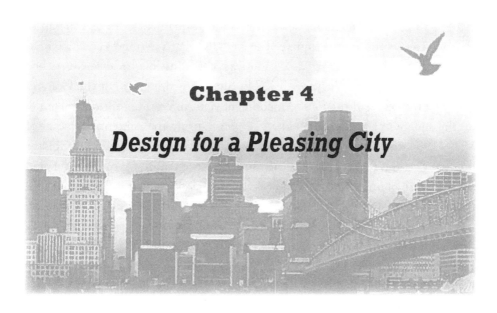

Chapter 4

Design for a Pleasing City

"A design for a pleasing city" was the rubric for the *City of Cincinnati 2000 Plan*, adopted in 1982. In late 1989, the City Council appointed a Plan Review Committee to "determine whether the City of Cincinnati is on target with downtown development outlined in the *Cincinnati 2000 Plan*" (City of Cincinnati Plan Review Committee, 1990, p. 1). With emphasis on the Central Business District (CBD), the Committee made its final report in December 2000, writing and reiterating throughout the report that

> the City Council and the City Manager must be unanimously convinced that a strong and vital [CBD] is a key part of their responsibility, and that a successful execution of the 2000 Plan will be good for every single citizen of Cincinnati, no matter where he or she may live. The City Administration and the entire Cincinnati community must strongly endorse this belief if success is to be achieved. (City of Cincinnati Plan Review Committee, 1990, p. 2)

These words written in late 1990 heralded a course of steady and unrelenting corporate and quasi-civic initiatives to promote business in the CBD and to remove those people, events, and influences seen as standing in the way of a "pleasing city." The area was viewed as a zone for the development of retail establishments, office space, and entertainment, especially in the area of the public square, anchored by the iconic Tyler Davidson Fountain, known as Fountain Square.

Recent history of the public space at Fountain Square includes several battles over "fighting words" on the Square. The Ku Klux Klan's permit to erect a Christian cross during the Christmas season was made possible because courts had previously found that Cincinnati's Rabbi Sholom Kalmonson, of the Congregation Lubavitch, had the First Amendment right to erect an 18-foot menorah on the square during the Hanukkah season. During the contentious years of 1989–1994, the city controlled and issued usage permits for Fountain Square, first denying the Rabbi's permit, then restoring the permit by court order, and subsequently permitting the Klan cross as well as the menorah and other religious symbols. In 1991, in an attempt to discourage religious displays, the City Council prohibited displays between 10 p.m. and 6 a.m., thereby requiring daily removal of crosses, menorahs, and even seasonal secular displays like the ballet's nutcracker or reindeer pulling sleighs. During the holiday season of 1992, Rabbi Kalmonson had challenged the ordinance in federal court. Judge Carl Rubin once more upheld free speech and once more clarified ownership of Fountain Square, declaring it a public asset:

> Ownership of that square always has rested in the citizens of Cincinnati, and subject to their right of use. Whether it is Congregation Lubavitch that seeks to exercise symbolic free speech by the display of a menorah or the Ku Klux Klan who wishes to spread its divisive message, the principle remains the same. (Margolick, 1992)

The CBD and the Fountain Square area provided a central venue for the previously described attempts to outlaw panhandling and remove panhandlers from public spaces in retail and office areas. In both the religious symbols and the panhandling cases, the court upheld First Amendment rights of free speech and required the city to issue permits for display of the symbols and to permit panhandling, respectively, within certain place and space limits.

At the time of the Plan Review Committee's report, the city blocks adjacent to Fountain Square had also been the location of several failed development projects proposing combinations of upscale retail space, office space, entertainment venues and hotels, and the nearby Convention Center, and these failures added urgency to review of the *City of Cincinnati 2000 Plan*. Details of these planning failures, often attributed to the departure of major department stores from the CBD, are beyond the scope of this study, but they provide contextual relevance to the direction heralded by the report: to surrender planning and development for the CBD to privatized, corporate structures soon to be developed (see Lebovitz & Salmon, 1999). The urgency of the work of economic development intensified, as it was seen as affecting the entire region and every citizen of Cincinnati.

The Plan Review Committee credited "remarkable progress on Office Buildings, Hotels, and the Convention Center" but discredited work on others areas of housing, riverfront development, parking and transportation, and environmental quality and urban design. Failures in these areas, called "deterrents" in the report, were attributed to lack of specific assigned responsibilities within city management; poor organization of city personnel; and "unavailability of enabling funds," cited as both investments of city capital funds and benefits from an infusion of resources generated by new businesses (City of Cincinnati Plan Review Committee, 1990, pp. 3–4). In short, the failures were failures of government, not business.

One of the key recommendations from the Plan Review Committee's work promoted the formation of an organized development or improvement district:

> The City should encourage for the longer term, the possible formation of a Business Improvement District to provide functions and services which significantly enhance the appeal of Downtown to all its users. The City should also encourage State legislation authorizing creation of a Business Improvement District and agree to maintain or increase downtown services and expenditures, is such a District is formed. (City of Cincinnati Plan Review Committee, 1990, p. 8)

By 1994, the city and business interests formed DCI, a nonprofit business organization incorporated and funded as a "Special Improvement District," using the newly formulated state codes for such organizations (State of Ohio, 2000). The district's geographical boundaries extended from the Ohio River on the south to the traditional West End at Central Avenue (including two city office buildings adjacent to City Hall) and to the traditional East End at Eggleston Avenue, with the northern boundary extended to Central Parkway, a major east–west thoroughfare. These parameters encompassed the downtown area, excepting the two major league baseball and football stadiums recently built or rebuilt on the riverfront, publicly financed for the Cincinnati Reds (Great American Ballpark, replacing Riverfront Stadium) and the Cincinnati Bengals (Paul Brown Stadium).

The mission of DCI (2009) was to "build a dynamic metropolitan center valued as the heart of the region" by providing the following services:

+ maintaining and enhancing a safe, clean, and welcoming environment downtown;

+ maintaining and enhancing the image, awareness, and usage of downtown as a vibrant hub of activity through strategic marketing and communications; and

+ advocating and supporting business and residential growth through stakeholder services programs.

The initial agreement between the city and DCI required that DCI maintain and promote Fountain Square and authorized the operation of vending programs on the Square. The agreement contained four elements: enhancing city cleaning and maintenance services; adding a "soft" security program using nonsworn, private staff; extending sidewalk vending and café activities onto the Square; and coordinating and consolidating management of special events and community uses of the Square (Cincinnati City Council, 1996a). A memo drafted by the director of public works and submitted by City Manager John F. Shirey (1996) to the Council, titled "Privatization of Fountain Square Management," pointed out that original proposals from DCI included transfer from the city to DCI of the responsibility for issuance of use permits for Fountain Square. At the time, using the existing policies, the Council majority retained the right to issue permits for events, rallies, demonstrations, and even display of religious symbols. The policies included regulations for use, noise, display size, and proximity to the Fountain; provision of city services; insurance coverage; prohibition of obscenity, defamation, and "fighting words"; and grievance procedures for denial of permits. This left the decisions on usage permits for all groups or users—whether the Ku Klux Klan's cross, the Rabbi's menorah, or the Horticulture Society's flowers—with the city, for the time being.

The soft security program using nonsworn, private staff included in the agreement was a euphemism for policing the Square. The security personnel were described in the manager's transmittal as "Community Service Representatives" who will serve as "City Ambassadors, uniformed and equipped with cellular phones to alert the police or cleaning crews" (Shirey, 1996). Although they had no police powers, these Ambassadors were generally viewed as security officers and were used as a cleaning crew, referral agents for social services, panhandler patrol, and ambassadors to the city for visitors. With an initial annual budget of $184,505 ($125,755 from the city, $12,500 from the Regional Transit Authority, and the balance from special events and vendor fees), this contract privatized management functions previously held by the city and surrendered management of public space from the city to a private corporation. The city did retain issuance of permits for events in this initial contract, maintaining public decision making on usage of this premier venue for public expression and free speech. The decision making for usage and "First Amendment functions" were subsequently transferred to a private purpose, and along with this transfer of decision making came the establishment of the larger development district known as Cincinnati Center City Development Corporation, Inc. (3CDC), discussed later. Because the city also retained full authority for safety services, hiring the Ambassadors resulted in no loss of police, firefighter, or public works jobs or employees.

Unlike some privatization initiatives that contract with for-profit companies for goods and services (for example, garbage collection, street repair, prison operation) undertaken in the name of saving public tax dollars and enhancing profits of private corporations, and unlike the selling off of public assets to private operation (for example, the Indiana Toll Road, public share of Conrail, timber rights to national forest land), the privatization of management of Fountain Square is a mixed model of contracting for certain services and control of public space. This model was undertaken for purposes of promoting business and preventing use by certain so-called undesirable people and events, supported by the idea that the strength of the entire city lies in the fortune of downtown business. According to DCI and other private interests, the fortunes of the entire region were somehow rooted in downtown economic development. As geographers Leibovitz and Salmon (1999) point out,

> In order to create a sense of urgency and "change attitudes," the DCI partnership employed a discourse of crisis. Whatever the objective "realities" of the Cincinnati situation, it was necessary to create the impression that immediate investment in the downtown redevelopment was necessary to avert economic decline. (p. 247)

With such impending crisis of economic decline, the course of crisis intervention to save downtown began with the privatization of Fountain Square management, which in many ways became the privatization of Fountain Square, shifting the city's focus of civic responsibilities from traditional metropolitan concerns of publicly shared space, service provision, and community development to a deliberate and nearly exclusive entrepreneurial concern for economic growth.

Chapter 5

Drug-Exclusion Ordinance

Although DCI's geographical boundaries were defined as the CBD, the lure of housing, entertainment/arts, and retail development opportunities began to extend to the adjacent community of OTR. In the 1990s, the population of OTR was fewer than 10,000, living in the oldest housing stock in the city (U.S. Census Bureau, 2000). Residents of OTR were plagued by the longstanding, severe household poverty of economic others, living with intractably high criminal activity driven largely by a market economy of drugs and prostitution, an economy purveyed by dealers and customers alike, most of whom were interlopers, not residents of OTR. The drug-exclusion ordinances described here were initiatives of DCI fully aligned with City Council members who had campaigned on anticrime, antidrug platforms. The ordinances were promoted to reduce crime but, in practice, removed people charged with drug and drug-related offenses, prior to judicial review, for purposes of "cleaning up" OTR for economic development.

Positioned as ridding OTR of its drug criminals, the initial exclusion ordinance targeted individuals who were mobile and transient within the community for purposes of commerce in drugs and prostitution. Like the Bavarian Law of 1926, intended to rid communities of Roma/Sinti groups, police-issued permits for exclusion from the community are found in Cincinnati's Drug-Exclusion Ordinance. Both laws concern exclusion of undesirable people from certain geographical areas, exclusion having been determined by police authorities without judicial review.

♦ From the Bavarian Law for the Combating of Gypsies, Travellers, and the Work-shy (July 16, 1926) (Burleigh & Wipperman, 1991):

   – Article 1: Gypsies and persons who roam about in the manner of Gypsies—"travelers"—may only itinerate with wagons and caravans if they have permission from the police authorities responsible. The permission may only be granted for a maximum of one calendar year and is revocable at all times. The license permitting them to do so is to be presented on demand to the [police] officers responsible. (p. 114)

   – Article 6: Gypsies and travellers may only encamp or park their wagons and caravans on open-air sites designated by the local police authorities, and only for a period of time specified by the local police authorities. (p. 115)

♦ From the City of Cincinnati Ordinance No. 229-1996 ordaining Drug-Exclusion Zones (Cincinnati City Council, 1996b):

   – §755-5 Civil Exclusion: A person is subject to exclusion for a period of ninety (90) days from the public streets, sidewalks, and other public ways in all drug-exclusion zones designated in Chapter 755 if that person has been arrested or otherwise taken into custody within any drug-exclusion zone for drug abuse or any drug abuse–related activities. [Nine offenses cited from the Ohio Revised Code Sections 2925.02, -.03, -.11, -.12, -.14, -.23, -.31, -.32, and -.37]

   – Additionally, any person arrested or otherwise taken into custody for any crimes listed above who is subsequently convicted thereof in a court of law for that offense is subject to exclusion for a one (1) year period from the date of such conviction from the public streets, sidewalk, and other public ways in all drug-exclusion zones designated in Chapter 755.

   – If the person excluded from a drug-exclusion zone is found therein during the exclusion period, that person is subject to immediate arrest for criminal trespass pursuant to Ohio Revised Code § 2911.21, a misdemeanor of the fourth degree.

   – §755-7 Issuance of Exclusion Notices: The chief of police is designated as the person in charge of the public streets, sidewalks, and public ways in drug-exclusion zones for purposes of issuing and directing the service of exclusion notices in accordance with this chapter.

The Bavarian Law was eventually enacted to take effect April 1, 1945; however, by 1945, the intent had changed from issuance of permits for removal by the police to incarceration of Gypsies and those who were "aliens to the community"

(Lewy, 2000), a category that included nonsedentary people who could not prove a regular source of income, sedentary individuals who made their living in illegal manner, the work-shy, and people whose way of life was seen as endangering the morals of other members of society.

As enacted by Cincinnati City Council, the Drug-Exclusion Ordinance similarly gave to the police authority for notice of exclusion of certain people from designated drug-exclusion zones, people whose activities were deemed to contribute to "the degradation of those areas and who adversely affect the overall quality of life for those areas' residents, businesses, and visitors." Per the ordinance, notice is given by police officers at time of arrest or citation and prior to arraignment or action of any judicial authority. This designation of specific geographical areas of the city as drug-exclusion zones, with exclusion of people arrested for illegal drug use and related activities, was modeled on the city's Panhandler Ordinances of 1995. However, unlike the Panhandler Ordinances, by this ordinance, codified in the city's Municipal Code as Chapter 755, authority was given to the police to issue notice of exclusion with limited procedures for appeal to the city's Safety Director and to issue written variance for presence in the exclusion zones for reasons relating to health, welfare, or well-being of the excluded person, such as drug abuse–related counseling services or social welfare services. In effect, this gave police authorities decision-making power outside the realm of police powers or responsibilities.

The initial exclusion zone was the OTR neighborhood adjacent to the CBD, making arrestees subject to exclusion from OTR for 90 days and for one year if convicted. Nine drug-related crimes were cited as subject to this civil exclusion, including possession, trafficking, abusing harmful intoxicants, and involvement with counterfeit controlled substances (all crimes codified in the Ohio Revised Code §2925).

Although the initial ordinance exclusively targeted the OTR community, it included provision for adding other communities. Incidence or concentration of drug-related activity, as worded in the Ordinance §755-1, were defined as occurring in

> those areas designated by the city council . . . where the number of arrests [for the listed crimes] and drug-abuse crimes for the twelve (12) month period preceding the original designation is significantly higher than that for other similarly situated/sized areas of the city.

The City Council also awarded itself the authority to remove such designations "in the event deemed not appropriate," but removal was to be accomplished by ordinance.

Like the Bavarian Law of 1926, the Drug-Exclusion Ordinance was enacted but did not withstand obvious and immediate contest in court. Suit was filed by the American Civil Liberties Union in the Hamilton County Court of Appeals on behalf of two individual arrested in OTR and notified of their exclusion. The court ruled that the Ordinance and Chapter 755 of the City Code were constitutional. The case was appealed in the United States District Court, which maintained that the law was unconstitutional. The city appealed to the Ohio Supreme Court in *State v. Burnett* (2001); the court found the ordinance unconstitutional on grounds of violating the guarantee of free travel afforded by the 14th Amendment to the United States Constitution as well as Ohio Constitution Section 3, Article XVIII, by adding penalty for violation of a state criminal statute not otherwise provided by the General Assembly (decided October 17, 2001, the appeal having come from Hamilton County Court of Appeals C-981003):

> We hold that chapter 755 of the Cincinnati Municipal Code is an unconstitutional violation of the right to travel as guaranteed by the Fourteenth Amendment to the United States constitution and a violation of Section 3, Article XVIII of the Ohio Constitution.

On appeal by the city of Cincinnati, the United States Supreme Court upheld the decision of the Ohio Supreme Court, rejecting the appeal without comment.

Although the Ordinance was in effect, other exclusion zones had been added to the Municipal Code, including Chapter 753, the Prostitution Exclusion Zone, and Chapter 757, the City Park Exclusion Zone. Nearly 11 years after enactment, as all exclusion zones were found unconstitutional by the Ohio Supreme Court and the Sixth Circuit Court of Appeals, and the United States Supreme Court had declined to hear appeals, the Cincinnati City Council repealed the exclusion zones provisions of the Code with Ordinance No. 178-2007, effective June 9, 2007.

Although these court decisions upheld the rights of all people, that a majority of Council could have enacted this Ordinance parallels the use of the Bavarian Law for Combating Gypsies, Travellers, and the Work-shy in the run-up to the Holocaust. In both of these laws, the intent shifted from punishment for crime, with the criminal act subject to judicial review, to punishment and banishment, ostensibly for purposes of protection of society. Like the Bavarian Law, the exclusion ordinances called for the

> incapacitation or removal of all "habitual criminals" defined as "the most dangerous element in this long chain of symptoms of social disease. Beggars

and vagabonds, prostitutes of both sexes, alcoholics, cheats and general members of the *demi-monde,* mentally and physically degenerates—they all form the army of fundamental opponents of the social order. (Wachsmann, 2001, pp. 166–167)

The ordinance was subsequently expanded beyond drug offenses to include offenses of prostitution and solicitation (targeting homosexual solicitation) in city parks (Chapters 753 and 757 of the Municipal Code, respectively), expanding the categories of excluded people to drug offenders, prostitutes, and sex solicitor, rather like the "beggars, vagabonds, prostitutes of both sexes, alcoholics, cheats and degenerates" of the Bavarian Law.

The policy justification for denying some individuals the right to be in certain zones was written into the ordinance as the city's compelling interest in restoring quality of life and protecting the health, safety, and welfare of citizens who use the public ways in drug-exclusion zones:

> The public interest in preventing the harmful effects of illegal drug abusers is so great that it justifies excluding those who engage in illegal drug abuse or illegal drug-abuse type criminal activity for 90 days from impacted areas in which they have engaged in or attempted to engage in illegal drug abuse-related activities. (§1 F)
>
> The city's health, safety, and welfare would best be served by temporarily excluding from impacted areas those persons who are arrested therein for illegal drug abuse or illegal drug abuse-related activity. (§1G)

The Cincinnati exclusion ordinances were repealed after facing judicial tests that preserved civil rights. In this instance, the balance between protection of the larger community from criminal activity and protections of civil rights was found in court, not in ordinance. But that is not the end of the story. Taken in a larger context of attempts by those in power to control and remove those without power, it presents alarming challenges to civil rights for individuals and to civil obligation to others in a humane, civil society. The toxic effect of these failed exclusion initiatives, sequentially following the Panhandler Ordinance, each a unitary policy-driven assault on economic others, heralded relentless, obdurate policy initiatives that extended for more than a decade in a larger story of econocide.

Chapter 6
Schools, Pools, Hoops, and Shelters

The unlikely intersection of school desegregation and shelters for homeless men, with pools and hoops between, has historical origins in 1973, when two organizations were founded that came to be major players in the drama to develop and gentrify OTR. The Cincinnati Public School for the Creative and Performing Arts (SCPA) and the DIC shelter for homeless adults were both established in 1973. Each was developed in response to cultural upheaval and policy shifts with major social justice implications, and both came to have enormous importance to economic development in OTR. Thirty years after founding, the school and the shelter were positioned against each other in a development battle in OTR surrounding the use of the city's 185 year-old, public Washington Park, located at their shared corner of 12th and Elm Streets. The school, the shelter, and the community were triangulated around who was entitled to use the park (neighborhood kids and economic others or new, affluent residents and arts supporters), what amenities were to remain in the park (swimming pools and basketball hoops or splash fountains and dog runs), and who could use privately held land owned by the DIC across 12th Street from the Park.

In 1973, the Cincinnati Public Schools responded to court-ordered desegregation of the schools by developing alternative, open-enrollment schools that came to be called "magnet" schools. In response to *Tina Deal, a minor, by Frank L. Deal, her father, et al., Plaintiffs v. The Cincinnati Board of Education et al.* (1965), the first of these schools, opened in the school year 1973–74 for grades 4 through

6, located in the existing Mt. Adams Elementary School. Other magnet schools framed around academic areas rather than enrollment by geographical boundaries that replicated segregation in housing soon followed—foreign languages, science and mathematics, physical education, college preparatory, Paideia and Montessori curricula—all advancing racial integration, though few had the wide appeal of SCPA. As upper and lower grades were added, SCPA grew to eight grades, consolidated in 1976 to one location in the former Woodward High School building at the eastern boundary of OTR. As of the 2010–11 school year, SCPA serves grades K–12 in a dazzling new building relocated in OTR, sharing the corner of 12th and Elm Streets with DIC and Washington Park, within a short city block from the magnificent landmark Music Hall, home of the Cincinnati Symphony Orchestra, the Cincinnati Opera, and the prestigious May Festival.

In 1973, DIC began to shelter homeless single men in OTR, many suffering from alcoholism and drug abuse, offering overnight shelter, food, treatment services, and safety from the streets. Whereas some clients were in need of detoxification and treatment, many needed only temporary shelter as they had been displaced from housing by the recent conversions of large apartment buildings in OTR. Many of these homeless single adults had previously been housed in rented SRO units in those large OTR buildings. In a dramatic housing shift, using newly available federal HUD financing, landlords converted buildings in OTR to rent-assisted units for economically eligible family tenants. Buildings that had previously housed single individuals in coldwater flats with sleeping rooms, shared bathrooms, and low weekly rental were now being converted, displacing single tenants, many of whom had lived in OTR their entire lives. By 1980, Tom Denhart, a landlord operating with an array of limited liability corporations, owned nearly 1,000 HUD-subsidized family units in dozens of OTR buildings.

Because there were no comparable SRO units on the market, many who were displaced by these HUD conversions had no alternative but DIC for shelter. In another federal public policy shift, with even more dramatic sequelae for urban neighborhoods than HUD conversions, in 1975 they were joined by hundreds, then several thousand single adults who were deinstitutionalized from state mental hospitals (Greater Cincinnati Coalition for the Homeless, 2001). These single adults were "returned to the community," few with any place but the DIC to escape living on the street or in public parks, sleeping in doorways or dumpsters. For many, escaping the street or dumpster was easier than finding treatment for the debilitating effects of mental illness, making DIC truly lifesaving.

By 1976, DIC had outgrown an apartment at Woodward and Main Streets, across a playground from the first OTR location of SCPA. Moving to the new

12th and Elm location meant DIC could serve its expanding clientele. Within two years of opening in the new location, DIC was serving as many as 250 people per day on average, fewer in warm weather, more during bitterly cold winter months. Many who need to use DIC may be described as economic others: single men and women, more than 60% with some income, mostly from hourly paid day labor, shutting most out of the housing market through their low or nonexistent incomes—that is, if they even could have found housing with rents comparable to those of SROs. Others suffered episodic crises precipitated by mental illness, substance abuse, or both, and many carried the stigma of old criminal records that precluded regular employment and housing. In many ways, those who need and use the DIC were, and remain to date, the most critically needy of the collectivity of economic others, because they do not qualify for categorical public assistance, employment training, or housing assistance.

By 1996, SCPA and DIC were drawn into a larger drama, reaching beyond meeting their respective social justice goals of educating children in desegregated schools and providing lifesaving shelter for homeless men. The flashpoint for this drama was implementation of the city's goal of economic development, advanced to ensure economic homogeneity in OTR. Plans for development of OTR included major renovation of Washington Park at the corner shared by SCPA and DIC. With full authority for OTR development handed off by city government to powerful, mainstream business interests, facilitated by newly organized public–private partnerships, the city's plan for a $16.7 million renovation of the park was described in the *Cincinnati Enquirer* as

> a relatively low-key redevelopment approach may be about to begin as private developers . . . prepare to launch a $16.7m redevelopment plan they hope will create an economic spark to help cure some of the ills that have plagued Over-the-Rhine. The Cincinnati Center City Development Corporation, known as 3CDC, has put together an acquisition and development plan it says could increase tax revenue for the city, spark consumer spending, create jobs and spur more private investment in the community. (M . M. Rose, 2006 p. A1)

These goals for redevelopment threw SCPA and DIC together in ways purported to be and publicized as a "cure for some of the ills that have plagued Over-the-Rhine."

For SCPA, the drama began with the organization of the GCAEC as a private, nonprofit organization, created to raise private-sector funds to build a new public SCPA in the vicinity of Music Hall, with the following mission statement:

> The mission of the Greater Cincinnati Arts and Education Center . . . is to create and support, in partnership with the Cincinnati Public Schools, a new K–12 School for Creative and Performing Arts near Music Hall. (http://www.222.thenewscpa.org/about/who.php)

Cincinnati Symphony Orchestra's assistant conductor, the late Eric Kunzel, brought visibility to GCAEC, adding his popularity as the conductor of the Cincinnati Pops Orchestra to fundraising and publicity for the new school. The GCAEC board was formed to include members who were among the most powerful leaders of the business community and significant contributors to the arts, clearly capable of raising private capital to match public funding as well as capturing all decision-making powers for this peculiar form of public–private partnership. The GCAEC mission coincided with Ohio's 1997 initiative "Rebuilding Ohio's Schools," which provided capital funds to school districts for building new schools and rehabilitating aging school buildings.

GCAEC proceeded with major fundraising efforts that joined identification of a site for the new school with efforts by others, particularly in the arts community, to save and renovate the city-owned, century-old Music Hall. GCAEC positioned its funding campaign with bold statements that the new school needed be near Music Hall, perhaps as close as next door. At the same time, discussions on the location for the new school soon included its proximity to the DIC and Washington Park, often by innuendo and foreboding statements about the behaviors of those who used Washington Park by day. This narrative became entangled with rehashing previously settled matters of panhandling, now singularly attributed to DIC and coupled with derisive narratives about "the homeless." Charges were made that DIC was the sole reason for panhandling as well as for crime and loitering by those who frequented Washington Park by day. Then-mayor Charlie Luken led the charge:

> The Drop Inn Center, the 22 year old homeless shelter for men in Over-the-Rhine, has become the latest combatant in the city's war against panhandling. Cincinnati Mayor Charlie Luken is insisting that the homeless shelter denounce panhandling by its residents and refuse services to people who commit crimes—such as improper solicitation—in downtown and Over-the-Rhine. (Korte, 2002b, p. B1)

There was never much evidence that park users were homeless, nor that they were more than occasional users of DIC.

As GCAEC began to raise money and received funding commitments from Ohio, the school board (responsible for all public schools) worked toward building and renovation plans for the entire district that included other public schools in OTR. The fate of Washington Park Elementary, located in the same block as the park, directly across from Music Hall, soon became ensnared in the decision making that had gradually been shifted from the public school board to powerful, privatized bodies—CGAEC and 3CDC.

By early 2003, the city had surrendered planning and development of the areas of OTR, downtown, and the banks to the newly formed private development corporation, 3CDC. Thus, a new player entered the drama that now surrounded plans for the school and, soon, the futures of DIC and Washington Park as well. 3CDC was authorized to find a site for the SCPA and to renovate the park, with full access to public funds from community development block grants (CDBGs), tax incentive financing (TIF), and tax credits and full operating responsibilities for the New Market Tax Credit Funds and Cincinnati Equity Fund (Cincinnati Center City Development Corporation, 2010a). By June 2006, 3CDC had rolled out a new plan that removed the elementary school from OTR, adding several acres to the footprint of the Park and using the school site for an underground parking garage, with an expansion of Washington Park at street level atop the garage. This swapping of space meant that the new SCPA building could be located on the block directly across Elm Street from the DIC and directly across 12th Street from Washington Park. Thus, DIC, SCPA, and Washington Park came to share the corner of 12th and Elm. The four corners hosted an empty, deteriorating Gothic church building that dates from the 1880s; the park, which had been there for a term measured in centuries; DIC, which was more than 30 years old; and SCPA, the newcomer.

As these plans were announced, press releases, memos, and news articles danced around the matter of removing DIC. The *Cincinnati Enquirer* praised the new plan, reporting the $52 million funding package was in place, including $26 million from the school district and the state; private funders, led by GCAEC, were to raise the matching $26 million. The *Enquirer* also reported that Joseph Pichler (retired CEO of the Kroger Company and chairman of 3CDC's OTR initiatives) stated that his 3CDC working group was "meeting with the Drop Inn Center officials to develop outreach programs to reduce crime in the area and keep Washington Park from being a hangout for the homeless" ("Good Plan for Washington Park," 2004, p. B14). The public narrative went something like this: *Those several dozen men and women who use the park by day—portrayed as derelicts, drunks, criminals, panhandlers, and "the homeless"—were too dangerous to be so close to a school, and they were there because of the DIC, so the DIC must be removed.*

DIC constituents, the OTR Community Council, OTR residents, and religious groups raised questions concerning the loss of the elementary school in OTR and challenged statements alleging that DIC was responsible for the neighborhood's crime, loitering, and use of the park. In June 2005, Pichler advised the board of the Metropolitan Area Religious Coalition of Cincinnati of the location for SCPA, that the elementary school would be moved, and that "we are working with the Drop Inn Center to find a new location" (Metropolitan Area Religious Coalition of Cincinnati, 2005).

When challenged, Pichler was given a pass about the DIC as he was overtly referring to three residential buildings owned by the DIC that had been renovated with HUD funds for transitional housing for 18 formerly homeless singles, located in the northwest corner of the block now identified for the new SCPA. The DIC and the school board were in close negotiations about the three buildings, especially since, by 3CDC's and GCAEC's latest plan, the school board needed the site. The board probably could have taken the three buildings by eminent domain. Alternatively, the DIC could have sold the buildings, but if it did not convert the buildings to retain their intended purposes as transitional housing, payback of HUD capital funds would be required. The DIC looked for alternative locations. Several sites in OTR were identified, each promptly and vigorously vetoed by 3CDC (Budzek, 2006).

At this point, the DIC had an option to purchase the recently vacated Samuel W. Bell Home for the Sightless, several blocks north of the DIC, just beyond Music Hall on Elm Street. The Bell Home building was ideal for institutional use, having been built with a single point of entry and individual rooms, intended as protective housing for the visually impaired and easily converted for those needing transitional housing with services. The school board did not claim eminent domain and prepared an alternative construction plan that did not include the three houses. Both the board and the DIC needed to resolve this 3CDC-triggered conundrum and the repeated vetoes of sites in OTR identified by the DIC.

The school board's construction deadlines were approaching; the DIC was frustrated dealing with 3CDC's stubborn resolve to deny purchase of the Bell Home. Resolution came when the DIC's option on the Bell Home property lapsed, and the DIC board offered the three houses on Elm Street to the school board at a fair price, relocating the housing units to McMicken Street in OTR, many blocks beyond Washington Park, not even close to the new SCPA, preserving services and meeting HUD requirements. SCPA's original architectural design was restored, and construction began, using the entire block for the school.

This was not to be the end of the story of the intersection of sheltering homeless singles and educating children in a desegregated school. The 2010–11 school year was the first year for SCPA in its new building serving children in grades K–12, and DIC continued to serve homeless adults, both located at the corner of 12th and Elm Streets at Washington Park. By May 2010, the DIC Board was summoned to City Hall for a meeting with the mayor, members of the City Council, the Continuum of Care, and 3CDC. The board was informed that DIC would be restructured, reduced in capacity, and removed from its 12th and Elm Streets location by 3CDC (Bernard-Kuhn, 2010). By mid-August 2010, 3CDC's plan to close Washington Park for renovation before the beginning of the school year was scheduled, and construction and grave removal begun behind fabric-covered chain link fences, angering OTR residents and community activists.

3CDC has had full authority for development of Washington Park since 2003. Early in 2009, a *Cincinnati Enquirer* series, "A Rare Change to Remake Over-the-Rhine" (Bernard-Kuhn, 2009b), profiled the accomplishments of 3CDC, including reference to planned renovations of Washington Park. Although the newspaper attributed planning to the park's owner, the Cincinnati Parks Department, rather than 3CDC, the planned changes included removing some people (economic others, the homeless, the mentally ill) while adding others (a backyard for residents affiliated with the arts):

> Cincinnati Park Department officials expect to resume planning by spring for a $14 million renovation of Washington Park.... Planners say the redesigned park will be the "backyard" for neighborhood residents, adjacent Music Hall, and the incoming School for Creative & Performing Arts.
>
> Why it matters: The project is a critical test for melding diverse interests. Planners say drastic measures are needed to clear crime from the park; others argue that the work is a veiled effort to hide Cincinnati's homeless and mentally ill who find refuge there. Some longtime residents also are fighting a plan to remove the park's deep-water pool. (Bernard-Kuhn, 2009b, p. F3)

References to clearing some people from the park and to keeping the deep-water swimming pool reflect community objections to the plan. Although there had been a series of public meetings, culminating in November 2007, to receive input from the neighborhood and local business interests on the proposed plan, to many it seemed that the ideas brought forward were ignored. Perhaps none were ignored as blatantly as retaining the City Recreation Commission's deep-water swimming pool and restoring basketball hoops. The plans called for removal of the deep-water pool, to be replaced with "spray ground" water features, and removal of the basketball hoops, to be replaced by a fenced-in dog run ("Save Pool, OTR Residents Say," 2007). The swimming pool (built in the 1970s with federal community development funds) had been used by the neighborhood for swimming lessons, for swim meets, and as an urban respite from summer's sweltering weather. At a contentious final meeting to receive input on the plan for the park, a petition was presented seeking to retain the pool and the hoops, signed by 400 residents of OTR. Considering that the population of OTR at the time had been reduced to fewer than 8,000, this represented substantial interest in plans for the park and presented a very different picture of residents' needs than what was repeatedly reported in news stories and presented in 3CDC's plan.

OTR residents were assisted in the petition drive to save the pool by students from Miami University's Center for Community Engagement in OTR (Flannery, 1997), who were enrolled in "studio courses" held in the urban neighborhood of OTR. The students—who were studying architecture, design, and planning—presented professional-quality alternative designs for the park, which were displayed at public meetings. Their work was based on interviews with residents and neighborhood constituents, research data obtained using current planning theory on urban parks, and data on water safety and drowning rates of those who had not learned to swim in childhood. The petition was ignored, and none of the proposals in the alternative plan were considered, not even open to discussion or negotiation.

In reporting on these public meetings held in November 2007, the *Cincinnati Post* focused on some of the elements of the plan and captured the negative, derisive sentiment surrounding park users, writing, "The park, known for drug busts, homeless inhabitants and crime, is seen as key to redevelopment in Over-the-Rhine" ("Save Pool, OTR Residents Say," 2007, p. 9); these negative perceptions about those who use the Park were perpetuated for years to follow. A letter to the editor of the *Cincinnati Enquirer* (Rotundo, 2010) some three years later opposed the planned changes, reflecting these competing urban interests:

Let neighbors keep their Washington Park.

The ongoing plans to redo Washington Park gave the appearance of a well-intended mindset. In reality, it may actually be a well-crafted transparency to allow the privileged and visitors to Music Hall to no longer see and vicariously experience the monotonous and grueling lives of the inner-city poor, the disenfranchised and eclectic souls to whom the current park serves as a safe haven and friendly place. To suggest that the alleged/proposed improvements like a spray park as opposed to a swimming pool are better insults the intelligence. Let's allow the locals to have their park as it is.

May the neighbors keep their Washington Park, for another century.

By late summer 2010, 3CDC had fenced off more than half of the park, shrouding it with a 12-inch opaque fabric to prevent viewing of construction and the archeological recovery of human remains from its previous use as a cemetery. Funding of $47.3 million was secured in a package that included city and state funds as well as TIF directed by the city of Cincinnati. A request for nearly $500,000 in annual operating subsidies was denied by the City Council, as the city faced a $50 million operating deficit for 2011. The full package includes an operations lease for the to-be-built below-ground garage; a lease for the above-ground space to construct improvements; a professional services agreement with the 3CDC subsidiary Washington Park Restoration, LLC, to operate and maintain the park; and related funding agreements to appear in biennial budgets. The term of agreement is 75 years, with two 10-year renewals for the garage; 60 years for the park; and an initial term of nine years with Washington Park Restoration, LLC, with subsequent "renewal options exercisable by the city" (Cincinnati City Council, 2010d). Private management of this public asset will continue for 95 years.

Within days of the execution of these agreements, fencing of the park restricted use but did not yet result in a complete shutout. Park users turned to the streets and other public spaces, many disappearing with the arrival of cold weather. The Greater Cincinnati Coalition for the Homeless pointed out, as the Community Council had previously suggested, that the proposed two-year construction schedule could have proceeded by section so that some areas of the park would always be available. At first, such obvious, sensible compromises fell on deaf ears as the developers and park managers wanted to implement a complete shutdown of the park. They eventually relented, leaving the southern section (closest to SCPA) open for use.

The shelter and the school are finding ways to coexist at 12th and Elm, below the radar of controversy. Overzealous police protection as school started in the fall was seemingly unnecessary, as school and shelter are now functioning side-by-side with no resultant calamities. The community was advised in early December 2010 that the park would be completely fenced by February 1, 2011, for two years. The irony of this episode is that although these arrangements and agreements were implemented to remove park users, especially economic others, in reality it was the park that was removed, so the park-users now could loiter and "chill" on sidewalks or in doorways and at the entrances of the businesses that had so rebuked them.

PART III

The City and Econocide: Cincinnati, Ohio, and Policy-driven Elimination of Affordable Housing

And homeless near a thousand homes I stood,
And near a thousand tables pined and wanted food.

—William Wordsworth,
Guilt and Sorrow; or, Incidents upon Salisbury Plain

Housing Occupancy in Over-the-Rhine, Census Year 2000

Total housing units	5,261
Vacant housing units	1,667
Total occupied units	3,594
Owner-occupied units	140
Renter-occupied units	3,454

—City of Cincinnati Planning Department,
Over-the-Rhine Comprehensive Plan, June 2002

Wordsworth's phrase "homeless near a thousand homes" is descriptive of a policy-driven reality of 21st century urban life in places such as the OTR community, as noted above, where an astonishing 1,667 of 5,261 (32% of all) housing units are vacant. Unlike policy efforts to remove panhandlers, beggars, alleged and convicted drug abusers, and solicitors of all sorts, another, more onerous kind of removal is found in a set of public policies directed at preventing development of and/or removing affordable housing from the market. This vicarious removal of some people—legally accomplished through legitimate legislative and administrative processes pertaining to housing subsidies, "land banking," zoning, and regulations/decisions on use of public funds—is equivalent to denying some members of the community access to the basic human need for a place to live.

The vacant housing in OTR counted in the 2000 Census had accumulated through a combination of the impending bankruptcy of the largest provider of subsidized units through HUD's "opt-out" option, buildings abandoned by absentee landlords, and an aging housing stock that had become increasingly difficult to maintain and heat. At the same time, housing and development policies driven by market economies came into direct conflict with grassroots, nonprofit housing development corporations attempting to save and rehabilitate affordable housing units. For-profit developers with the capacity to raise capital were lured by low-cost investment opportunities in OTR, acquiring aging buildings with historic designations in prime locations in proximity to the CBD as well as existing arts and entertainment venues. Simultaneously, market-driven policies reduced government budgets and jeopardized publicly funded assistance programs related to housing development and subsidies for economically eligible households that neighborhood-based nonprofits had accessed for decades.

Shortages of affordable housing and reduced housing assistance funds are major precipitants of homelessness. A working definition of *affordability of housing* originates with HUD and is framed to reflect household income:

> The generally accepted definition of affordability is for a household to pay no more than 30 percent of its annual income on housing. Families who pay more than 30 percent of their income for housing are considered cost burdened and may have difficulty affording necessities such as food, clothing, transportation and medical care. (HUD, 2009)

HUD further establishes fair market rents (FMRs) for each statistically identifiable region of the country. FMRs and the 30 percent affordability rule of thumb are an impossible combination for low- or no-income households, and especially economic others. Thirty percent of the minimal, irregular incomes (or no incomes) earned by economic others comes nowhere near FMR rent levels, and reduced housing assistance funds means reduced rental assistance as well as reductions in units available in the market. These concepts of affordability and FMR rents have meaning only when affordable units are available—that is, not withheld from the market.

Examples of housing and development policies in recent experience in the city of Cincinnati that reduced, blocked, or eliminated affordable rental units and housing development are described here. These examples are presented to illustrate ways that policy decisions contribute to the econocide of economic others who have no or limited access to housing. These stories are chronologically overlapping, with some policy issues heralding subsequent ordinances, resolutions, and administrative acts, but in the end are quilted with the same thread into relentless policy attacks on economic others as part of an astonishing, policy-driven econocide.

Beginning with the demise of the Vine Street Community Project, initiated by the OTR grassroots community development corporation (CDC) known as "ReStoc," and proceeding through city and federal policy shifts reducing availability of affordable housing, the policies considered here, unlike the policies to directly remove economic others as individuals, promote indirect removal of economic others by removing housing from the market. Simultaneous shifts in housing assistance policies exclude many economic others from participation in assistance programs. The policies to be considered are as follows:

+ the OTR Vine Street Community Project Tax Credit Project rejection (2000);
+ the Housing Impaction Ordinance (No. 346-2001) (2001);
+ the Hope VI HUD to replace Public Housing Projects (2001);
+ the HUD policy shift from project-based subsidies to HCVs, previously known as Section 8 vouchers; and
+ the de facto eminent domain bankruptcy sale of Denhart Properties (2,051 privately held and operated units of subsidized housing moved "to the market").

These policies illustrate another chapter of contemporary econocide in which policy decisions result in a deliberately contrived scarcity of affordable housing.

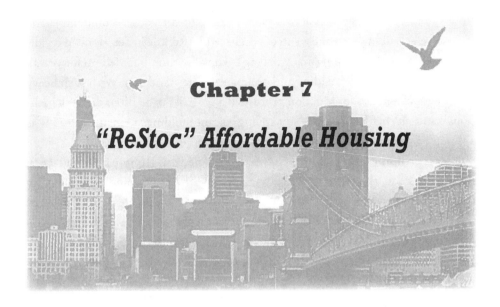

Chapter 7
"ReStoc" Affordable Housing

The Race Street Tenant Organization Cooperative (ReStoc) was organized in 1978 in OTR as a nonprofit housing development corporation with the straightforward mission "to ensure the availability of affordable housing in a community environment." An outgrowth of the DIC, the city's largest homeless shelter for singles, ReStoc initially focused exclusively on development of SRO units for the purpose of providing affordable, permanent housing to single people at affordable rents. These one-room units were of small size, with "small" rents. Tenants were drawn from the DIC's homeless clients—mostly single men, many in recovery, most working, some disabled, many working *and* disabled. Almost all of these SRO tenants were economic others who had been driven from housing by the conversion of many former SRO buildings to family rental units in HUD programs originating in the 1970s, many of these the same buildings subsequently "opted-out" of HUD subsidy programs.

Operating as a tenant cooperative, ReStoc was deliberate about promoting community control, racial and economic diversity, and self-determination in meeting housing needs. ReStoc's board, known as the "Board of Owners," required 51 percent tenant membership. The mission deliberately included a mandate to advocate for affordable housing, especially in the OTR community.

Ten years after its founding, ReStoc had completed more than 100 units, using public funds, private donations, and an extraordinary amount of volunteer labor (high school service learners, civic groups, fraternities, labor unions, clubs, church groups) and volunteer professionals (architects, skilled trades, accountants). The units were in buildings no one wanted, purchased by ReStoc in deteriorated condition, saved from demolition (many having been vacant and boarded up for years), and restored to meet all building and occupancy code standards. With such heavy reliance on volunteers, production proceeded at a snail's pace, often drawing malicious criticism that ReStoc was "stockpiling" vacant buildings to maintain OTR as a "dumping ground for the poor" ("Housing in Over-the-Rhine," 2000).

Because the buildings were legitimately owned by ReStoc and had been restored to code, the criticism of vacancy became the only point of attack. City Council member Jim Tarbell, a long-time advocate for upscale development of OTR, voiced this kind of criticism, proposing that the city be prohibited from using funds to develop Vine Street, the main north–south thoroughfare in OTR. Supposedly the market would do it and "ultimately involve the city using its power to condemn buildings that sit vacant in order to assume ownership and sell the properties for redevelopment" (Osborne, 2000b, p. 10A). This kind of threat was perceived by ReStoc as "land grabbing"—confiscating legitimately owned property by using powers of government for subsequent sale to developers for usage certain to deny housing to economic others.

By the mid-1990s, under fire of relentless accusations of "stockpiling" buildings and with slow production rates renovating their own buildings and growing demand for affordable housing, the ReStoc board made a major change in their mission, shifting from SRO units only to family units. Using eight vacant buildings in proximity to 12th and Vine Streets, owned either by ReStoc or the DIC, ReStoc proposed a 45-unit project consisting of one studio, 17 one-bedroom, 10 two-bedroom, 13 three-bedroom, and four four-bedroom units, all to be rented at affordable rates. This enormous leap in production and shift to family units was named the "Vine Street Community Project." ReStoc secured funding in the amount of $5.09 million through the Low Income Housing Tax Credit program, Ohio housing funds, the Cincinnati Development Fund, and the city's HOME funds. This complex funding package was the largest project ever undertaken by ReStoc.

The funding package was completed in February 2000, with the majority of funds in the amount of $4,054,630 coming from a competitive proposal made for Ohio Low Income Housing Tax Credit funding and with preliminary approval in the Housing Round VII for the HOME fund to be approved by the city of Cincinnati for $700,000. The Ohio Low Income Housing Tax Credit proposal was competitive, with ReStoc's proposal ranking third among 65 proposals in the state. The total package for $5,095,630 included a small city grant of $35,000 for façade improvement for the buildings facing Vine Street, including 1214 Vine Street, a historic, classic Italianate building with beautiful carved stone cornices. To complete the funding package and meet all deadlines for the several funders, final approval for the HOME funds of $700,000 was to come before City Council in June 2000. The project had a deadline to begin construction by the end of 2000. No objections had been raised by the city about the project, which had the approval of Mayor Charlie Luken, who had previously endorsed the HOME funds in writing, citing the project's consistency with the city's HUD-required and approved Consolidated Plan. Luken also noted that 30,000 units of affordable housing were needed during the five-year term of the plan. This project would add 45 units.

Approval of the $700,000 was never to come. Private developers who were beginning to work on upscale condominiums and home ownership had targeted OTR for development and wanted 1214 Vine Street for its lovely façade and "plum" location. The mayor withdrew his approval, the City Council deadlocked 4–4 on the issue, and the fight was on, pitting ReStoc and the OTR community against developers, whose battle was fronted by city government in the name of "more market-rate properties needed to revitalize the struggling neighborhood" (Osborne, 2000a, p. 15A).

The visible battle was fought in public, in hearings, but most of all in the press. The city offered a "take it or leave it" proposal to ReStoc to surrender (sell to developers) 1214 Vine Street for market-rate development; to reduce the number of units from 45 to 30; and, in a strategy to remove undesirable renters (economic others), to reconfigure the rents in the remaining units, tipping the balance to "higher allowable rent range and fewer in the range for very low income persons" (Riordan, 2002). The negotiations were complicated by simultaneous renegotiations with the other funders (for example, Ohio Low Income Housing Tax Credit) as the funding package collapsed, and the sale of the 1214 property was demanded. All of these changes necessitated legal services for ReStoc. To raise funds to pay for legal services, related title searches, and environmental impact certifications, ReStoc was forced to sell another building, as no pro bono legal services could be arranged for this unexpected situation.

A *Cincinnati Post* editorial position summarized and supported the position of the developers and what was soon to be a majority of the City Council, citing the issue as "a legacy of the days when the city's policy was to concentrate poor people and social service agencies there [in OTR] in hopes of keeping blight from spreading to other neighborhoods" ("Housing in Over-the-Rhine," 2000, p. 16A). The editorial continued:

Civic, business, political and other interests eager to revitalize Over-the-Rhine have long complained that ReStoc has failed to carry out promises to renovate the properties it owns, charging that it prefers instead to warehouse the buildings and resist gentrification of the neighborhood. . . . The project would continue the practice of concentrating low-income housing, and it would discourage the development of market-rate housing or other projects along Vine Street. . . . The city's goal should be to encourage preservation and rehabilitation of its marvelous housing stock . . . that goal won't be met, however, if council allows social service agencies—no matter how well intentioned–to preserve Over-the-Rhine's status as a dumping ground for the poor. (p. 16A)

When the vote finally came to City Council, the Vine Street Community Project was denied the $700,000, and the project was lost. Betrayed by Mayor Luken, ReStoc had no choice but to "negotiate" the smaller project, selling 1214 Vine Street to the Cincinnati Development Fund and reconfiguring the project to fewer units with higher rents that would preclude renting to economic others. The reconfiguration of the project drastically changed and delayed it, with final contracts not in place until January 2002; construction did not begin until March 2002, nearly four years after original written approval for its funding.

At the time of the defeat of the 45-unit project, a *Cincinnati Enquirer* report cited City Council members as saying "there is already too much low-income housing in Over-the-Rhine and it is inhibiting revitalization efforts" (Anglen, 2000, p. C1). Further, the *Enquirer* positioned the story to describe ReStoc as not a housing developer but a social service agency, heralding an additional dynamic to the soon-to-emerge "concentration of poverty" arguments *against* OTR (paired with the "concentration of social services" *in* OTR), impeding development and revitalization. By the time the contracts for the Vine Street Community Project were finalized in November 2000, the city's planning director Liz Blume announced that the scheduled meetings to develop a new OTR master plan were proceeding. In an *Enquirer* article wryly titled "Is Over-the-Rhine Ripe for Development?" Blume is credited with indicating that the

city is committed to revitalizing the section of Vine Street between Central Parkway and Liberty [geographically inclusive of the Vine Street Community Project properties]. . . . and plans to add $4 million to the housing budget in 2001 to fund more market-rate development citywide. (Alltucker, 2000).

ReStoc's forced compromise in its battle for affordable housing reduced proposed units by 15—small in number but huge in significance in shifting power in OTR from public support for community self-determination to an ideology of development in a market economy. The significance of this power shift could only be imagined at the time but soon emerged in the following parts of this story of policy decisions pertaining to housing, positioned with so-called "concentration of poverty linked with over-saturation of subsidized housing, that taxes too strongly city services, creating a domino effect of declining property values relative to inflation and increasing social ills" (Cranley, 2001b).

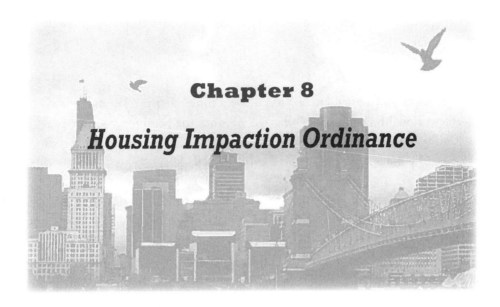

Chapter 8

Housing Impaction Ordinance

By the time ReStoc signed the contracts for the smaller Vine Street Community Project, another policy-driven obstacle to development of affordable housing in communities like OTR had been enacted during the City Council election year of 2001. Councilmember John Cranley (part of the Council's Democratic majority), who had been appointed to fill a vacancy late in 2000, proposed and vigorously moved toward adoption an ordinance that became known as the Housing Impaction Ordinance (Cincinnati City Council, 2001). The substance of the Ordinance is found its the opening wording:

> Declaring the policy of the City of Cincinnati in the budgeting and expenditure of Community Development Block Grant and HOME Investment Partnership Program funds and in the approval of low income tax credit projects to support homeownership, reduce the concentration of poverty, rehabilitate vacant and abandoned buildings, preserve and improve affordable housing and oppose the construction of new publicly-assisted low-income rental units unless the construction reduces the concentration of poverty. (Cincinnati City Council, 2001)

The two "whereas" clauses of the Ordinance are as follows:

WHEREAS, Council desires to promote livable neighborhoods for everyone, promote mixed-income neighborhoods, preserve and improve the

City's affordable housing stock, expand choice for participants in public housing;

and

WHEREAS, Council intends to pursue a comprehensive fair and affordable regional housing policy that will advance the common good by promoting a preferential option for enhanced housing opportunities for all, especially the poorest. (Cincinnati City Council, 2001)

Operative words in the ordinance make it the policy of the city to "reduce the concentration of poverty" pertaining to use of city, federal, and Low Income Housing Tax Credit funding for housing and economic development. The ordinance makes no mention of expanding or replacing affordable housing options, except for this clause: "expand choice for participants in public housing" (Cincinnati City Council, 2001). At the time, the Public Housing Authority was engaged in the federally sponsored Hope VI project to demolish obsolete but livable 1930s project-style buildings, replacing them with modern townhouses. That plan actually resulted in a reduction of the number of affordable units for eligible tenants.

The second "whereas" clause of the ordinance, referencing a regional housing policy, is a residual from early drafts that would have precluded use of city-directed funds within the city until concentrations of poverty in the city were reduced or other jurisdictions bore a greater share of affordable units. The latter idea was promptly quashed by adjacent municipalities and townships, who claimed that lowered property values, blight, and increased crime would follow should they be besieged by such housing. They joined proponents of affordable housing to complain at divisive, sometime raucous City Council hearings on the ordinance. One township trustee claimed that the city was "trying to kick low-income housing issues down suburban throats." Advocates for retaining the city's funds for affordable housing development in the city claimed that the ordinance was just "a kinder, gentler way of saying 'no more poor people'" (Anglen, 2001, p. BX). The *Cincinnati Enquirer* editorial position, run under the title "Ban Low-Income Rentals, Middle Class Flight" (2001), gives voice to the dichotomous issue: "Vocal opposition splits into two groups: Suburbanites want to keep low-income housing out of their neighborhoods; inner-city activists claim it's an "ethnic cleansing" plot to remove poor folks from Over-the-Rhine" (p. B10). The Housing Impaction Ordinance was enacted October 31, 2001. Although referencing policies to "encourage the development of housing choices for people of all income levels throughout the region," it codifies substantial impediments to rehabilitation and development of affordable housing in poor communities in the city.

During the "selling" of the ordinance to the community and the drafting of the final legislation, the sponsors of the ordinance did not refer the draft to the city's administration for review but, rather, began a campaign to move toward adoption prior to the Council election of November 2001. In one public meeting, councilmember Cranley, who had authored the ordinance, was challenged by housing activists to state how it conformed to the city's HUD-approved *Consolidated Plan* (Cincinnati City Council, 2004a, 2004b, 2004c). He claimed with certainty that the ordinance would conform, although the next day he is reported to have phoned the city Budget Office with a request for a copy of the *Plan*. Subsequently, key city administrators, Finance Director William Moller and Director of Neighborhood Services Peg Moertl, provided a critical review of the proposed text (Moller & Moertl, 2001).

Moller and Moertl advised that the intentions of the ordinance directed toward home ownership were better fit for a resolution, not an ordinance, as key program elements were already covered through other programs (for example, down payment assistance, low-cost rehabilitation loans, lead abatement) in approved CDBG funds. The directors, who would be charged with implementation of the ordinance, pointed out that it referenced poverty and low-income housing without specific definitions. They recommended that a definition of household poverty, for purposes of the ordinance, be 30 percent of the area's median income, as in HUD's definition of low-income families. They also advised that the ordinance, if adopted, would require amendment to the city's HUD-approved *Consolidated Plan* as the ordinance represented substantial change in the allocation and selection criteria approved in the currently adopted plan. Approval of such changes requires an open process of review by advisory bodies, a 30-day period for comment, a public hearing on the changes, and action by City Council to amend the *Plan*. Without such amendment, the city could be subject to HUD audit findings for allocations in violation of the *Consolidated Plan*.

Although this was a contentious issue concerning policies for the funding of affordable housing, a more subtle text in the discussion was the introduction of the concept of *concentrated poverty*, and the supposed urgency to "deconcentrate" it, into public discourse on housing in Cincinnati. By 2000, although these concepts were new to public discourse on housing and development in Cincinnati, scholars and researchers had been studying concentration of poverty in a discussion that most likely began when William Julius Wilson (1987) reframed and expanded Gunnar Myrdal's concept of the underclass (Wilson, 1987). Wilson's work described people in an "urban underclass" who were economically and socially isolated by phenomena of structural nature: restructured economic realities, especially in employment and loss of jobs in urban areas. Study of the underclass as a social phenomenon began to shift from sociological description and theorization pertaining to demographics and geographic isolation of poor people to behaviors of members of the underclass. In this instance, the behaviors were often described with a "moral spin"—dropping out of school, bearing children out of wedlock, being work-shy and welfare dependent. Wilson related underclass behaviors to concentrations of poverty, particularly of African American families, thereby broadening the discussion to include race.

According to some researchers (Goetz, 2000; Jargowsky, 2003), Wilson's work generated several tracks for exploration of determinants of concentrated poverty: continued study of structural economic elements, shift from industrial to high-tech jobs, entrapment of poor populations in urban areas, and flight of employers from urban to suburban areas distanced from the urban poor. Attendant research areas, often related to federal policies, included housing, especially public and subsidized housing; racial segregation; fair housing; family formation, particularly single-parent, female-headed households; public assistance; and young African American men supposedly responsible for escalating crime in urban areas (Goetz, 2000; O'Connor, 2001).

Federal policy changes pertaining to housing in the 1990s, especially those including notions of concentrated poverty, had impact on cities like Cincinnati with dense urban areas, old housing stock, deteriorating 1930s public housing projects, and escalating rates of crime attributed to poor communities being havens for drugs and prostitution. These changes were driven by what Goetz (2004) calls "a moral panic" over crime in central cities that affected the availability of affordable housing, especially housing that was public and subsidized. Goetz (2004) cites programs like HUD's Weed and Seed (weed the criminals, seed the housing), Move to Opportunity (promote home ownership), and Hope VI (remove tenants, demolish public housing projects), all aimed at removing economic others, especially criminals and those with social pathologies, including many who qualified economically for housing assistance:

> Our preoccupation with the criminal threat of low-income inner-city residents reinforced the impulse to disperse the poor. The physical decay of public housing suggested an urban renewal approach that would remake central city neighborhoods, simultaneously forcing the removal of the existing population. Because this population was politically weak, it was unlikely

to mount an effective defense against such measures. So it was that deconcentration manifested itself as the demolition of poor people's homes and
their forced removal from the communities they lived in. (para.17)

Although Goetz frames deconcentration as originating in an escalating fear of
crime, the Cincinnati discourse on concentration of poverty came to be framed by
a sequence of policies pertaining to use of public funding for affordable housing,
economic development, and housing rehabilitation, thereby shifting the discourse
and legislation from blatant removal of economic others to removal of their housing options.

The Housing Impaction Ordinance, as introduced and enacted, provided a
grim description of so-called impacted neighborhoods but was not linked specifically to crime (perhaps excluding crime because the previous Drug-Exclusion
Ordinance had failed as public policy). Instead, it required city administration
to identify neighborhoods "impacted by an over-saturation of low-income residents, judged by median income, reliance on public subsidy and property values"
(Cincinnati City Council, 2001). At the time, most researchers had come to use
Danziger and Gottschalk's (as detailed in Goetz, 2003) operating definition of
concentration of poverty as "neighborhoods identified by Census Tract(s) with
more than 40% of the population living below the poverty level" (p. 25). (This
is different from the HUD definition of low income as below 30 percent of an
area's median income). The Cincinnati ordinance used still a different definition, citing demographics of certain census tracts but adding property values
and incomes from public assistance as the measure of concentration of poverty.
Residents, "concentrated" in neighborhoods identified by their income level and/
or use of public subsidies, were deemed to be the cause of the problems the
ordinance purported to eliminate. The same kind of banal terminology might
easily have been used had the identified problem been an invasion of predatory
pests—concentrations of feral dogs or disease-bearing rats—to be removed for
prevention of rabies or other contagion.

Previously, the city's formulations of housing problems were made through
descriptions of conditions such as age or deterioration of housing stock, density
of population, funding availability, environmental contamination, or historic designation, but rarely—if ever—by judgments of residents' standards of income
(below median) or reliance on public subsidy (welfare, housing subsidies). This
shorthand for those economic others who somehow concentrated themselves in
poor neighborhoods came to dominate public discourse on housing policy. The
ordinance provided the solution to these supposedly resident-caused housing

problems by preventing public spending on affordable housing development and changing zoning codes to favor home ownership.

In a memorandum to the mayor and the City Council (Cranley, 2001a) Councilmember Cranley's justification for the Housing Impaction Ordinance poses what he calls a "binary debate" that "pits safe and viable neighborhoods against the needs of those who need affordable housing." He continues:

> Middle class neighborhoods do not want affordable housing viewed as a spark of a downward trend . . . in fear born of iconic imagery of highly concentrated projects moving into their neighborhoods with run-down property resulting from neglect or slumlord practices. Concentrating poverty emerged as a way to advance these two concerns—a moral goal (housing for those who need it) and a policy necessity (preserving the viability of middle class neighborhoods). Against this backdrop, de-concentrating poverty seems to be an unworkable binary choice. Cynically, it seems the city must choose between safe neighborhoods or a commitment to the provision of affordable housing. (Cranley, 2001a)

The solution to this binary debate was to deny public funds for housing in neighborhoods with "concentrated poverty," using funds only to reduce or "deconcentrate" poverty. It is a curiously unitary position, with no "exit plan" for those being deconcentrated.

Further, the dichotomous debate of deconcentrating the poor (removing economic others) without peril (reducing property values, increasing crime) to nonpoor and suburban communities entangled discourse. Underlying assumptions that concentrated poverty is bad and requires deconcentration, and that deconcentrated poverty directly undermines property values in "nonpoor" areas and should be forbidden, became so enmeshed that both proponents and opponents of deconcentration were propelled to the same position of opposing the ordinance.

As a housing policy response to the problem of concentrated poverty, the Housing Impaction Ordinance is deeply flawed. A plan for deconcentrating poverty by means of provision for affordable housing for real people, not some mass to be deconcentrated, is missing. Although the action proposed in the ordinance was to deconcentrate poverty, it blocked new initiatives that required public funds for maintaining and rehabilitating affordable units in the same neighborhoods, and it prohibited replacement or additional units in other neighborhoods. However, it did preserve empty buildings "land-banked" for future use, especially those in prized historic districts like OTR, making them available for upscale development that purportedly did not seek or require public funding.

If the Housing Impaction Ordinance is viewed as an antipoverty policy, as it proposed to reduce concentrations of poverty, it is equally flawed. Reduction of poverty requires a broader approach, as Goetz's (2003) studies of initiatives to deconcentrate poverty in public and subsidized housing in Minneapolis, Minnesota, demonstrate. These studies speak to the limitations of a narrow approach of using housing without other simultaneous initiatives:

> A responsible antipoverty policy should not lead with the demolition of low-cost housing and the forced relocation of the poor. This nation's history with the urban renewal program suggests that without complementary actions to reduce exclusionary barriers and incentives that foster and facilitate growing socioeconomic disparities—and the geographic expression of those disparities—the scattering of poor people, in itself, accomplishes little. (Goetz, 2003, p. 256)

The narrow approach of the Housing Impaction Ordinance indirectly forces relocation of the poor, with no complementary location; it scatters them to places that only exacerbate their economic otherness, or to nowhere.

If the Housing Impaction Ordinance is seen as an economic development policy, it is flawless. It effectively blocks development or rehabilitation of affordable housing units in areas deemed to be concentrated with poverty, effectively keeping affordable units for economic others off the market. Most of the housing serving economic other families and individuals in OTR is developed by local, nonprofit development corporations. Their properties and holdings are located in areas coveted by developers—historic district designations, prestigious arts venues, areas adjacent to the CBD—matching the real estate development ideal of "location, location, location." In many ways, the Housing Impaction Ordinance, as an economic development policy, serves as privatization of public policies of eminent domain—de facto eminent domain. City government needs initiate no policy action to take buildings to serve city goals of increasing private development; the ordinance accomplishes that. Further, as buildings in the affected neighborhoods "concentrated" with poverty are deteriorating, boarded, or empty, they were prime targets for developers, many of whom had urged adoption of the ordinance. Market developers can now step in to "buy low" and "rehab high," simultaneously blocking the market for affordable housing by eliminating places where economic others could live and deconcentrating poverty.

Chapter 9

Hope VI: There Were Not Enough Houses for Us to Live In

Our defenseless eyes cloud with bewilderment when we learn that there are not enough houses for us to live in. And competing with us for shelter are thousands of poor migrant whites who have come up from the south just as we have come.... The tenements we live in are old; they are rarely repaired or replaced. On most of our buildings are signs: THIS PROPERTY FOR SALE. Any day we can be told to move, that our home is to be torn down to make way for a new factory or a new mill.

—Richard Wright, *12 Million Black Voices*

Richard Wright's description of the experiences of black Americans who came to northern cities in what was known as the Great Migration (1916–1970) provides insight into the origins of public housing policy in 20th century America. Wright's account describes experiences in Chicago, but it could easily be Cincinnati, Detroit, Cleveland, or any industrial city of the Midwest where black migrants to the industrial North found scarcity of housing; competition with other poor populations for it; racial discrimination in renting; and flight of mostly ethnic, white landowners from their homes, now turned into tenements.

In Cincinnati, many black and poor white populations who migrated to the city sought and found housing in the West End neighborhood, located geographically in the basin area adjacent to OTR and the CBD. Like the areas of Chicago described by Wright, the West End had come to be the area with the densest population, highest crime rates, and most deteriorated buildings in the city. Housing stock that had been home to and owned by German and Italian immigrant populations of the 19th century was now subdivided into small units, rented to mostly black tenants as the owners moved to more desirable hilltop locations. In pre-Depression years, it was a slum of textbook specimen quality.

The West End was to become home to two huge Work Projects Administration (WPA) projects—the glorious art deco Union Terminal train station and major slum clearance for two public housing projects. The Laurel Homes project was built in 1938 to house 1,303 white households, and Lincoln Court was built in 1942 to house 1,015 black households. The story of the late-20th-century Hope VI initiatives of the QHWRA really begins with these first West End projects that were built to clear slums and provide modern, low-cost housing. By the late 20th century, both projects themselves had been demolished in the name of "slum clearance" to remove "severely distressed public housing projects" in a program known by the euphemism "Hope VI."

Historian David Stradling (2003) describes the pre-Depression West End as the most crime ridden area of the city, which ranked above the national average in murders (75) and aggravated assaults (411) annually: "More than 70% of the murders occurred in the basin, particularly in the West End, as did more than 75% of the aggravated assaults. Statistics revealed the concentration of crime in densely populated black neighborhoods" (p. 109).

Like the Union Terminal project, the housing/slum clearance projects were reported in the WPA (1943) *Writers Guide:* "People were leaving the crowded, decrepit West End, but its battered rooming houses and slums remained unchanged. With the completion in 1933 of the huge Union Terminal project, a slum clearance program seemed in order for the West End" (p. 132). And so it was that the city sought to participate in the massive Federal Housing Authority initiatives to clear the slums and provide low-cost housing for the West End population. The magnificent Union Terminal was spared both subsequent slum clearance and later "urban renewal" to be renovated as the Museum Center, which included the Historical Society, Natural History Museum, Children's Museum, and IMAX Theatre.

The CMHA was created in 1933 to build these West End projects and others in the region. A meticulously documented account of the organization of CMHA in response not only to slum clearance, but also to progressive notions of fair housing and economic development, is found in Robert A. Fairbanks's (1988) *Making Better Citizens: Housing Reform and the Community Development Strategy in Cincinnati, 1890–1960* (see pp. 71–88). The two huge housing projects that were built in the West End accommodated to the distortions of segregation in the city's real estate environment. In 1921, the Cincinnati Real Estate Board had adopted the following policy: "No agent shall rent or sell property to colored [*sic*] in an established white section or neighborhood and this inhibition shall be particularly applicable to the hilltops and suburban property" (Stradling, 2003, p. 110).

Although this was a Real Estate Board policy, not a City Code, it reflected both sentiment and practice in the city. However, the same notions were reflected a few years later in the city's 1925 *Official Plan of Cincinnati, Ohio* (City of Cincinnati Planning Commission, 1925), reputed to be the first city master plan in the country. The *Official Plan* was written and codified to address public matters of community development, zoning, transportation, parks, schools, garbage and refuse removal, and "subdivisions and housing." By ordinance, the *Plan* became the official code of the city. Under the title "Housing Problems in Cincinnati," the *Plan* describes the housing situation "so far as wage earners are concerned" as more pressing than at any previous time, due to few housing vacancies, overcrowding, and increasing rent levels in the tenements. Eighty percent of the tenements in the city were in the West End. The plan references the difficulties reported by social agencies in providing satisfactory solutions to family problems that they sought to "adjust" as being due to the housing conditions. Not stopping at placing the problems with the tenant families, the *Plan* continues as follows:

> The colored [*sic*] population is continuing to increase fairly rapidly, while the number of houses is remaining stationary. Nearly 3,500 new colored people have come into Cincinnati since 1920. This is bound to remain a problem for several decades to come.... Eighty percent of the tenements are in the "Basin" [the West End is so named as it is the west end of the "basin"]. Fortunately from the standpoint of sanitation, the population of the "Basin" is decreasing due to their being forced out by the spread of industry and business. However, for the last two years this decrease has been counteracted by the unusual influx of colored people. (City of Cincinnati Planning Commission, 1925, pp. 50–51)

In but a few short sentences, the housing problem in Cincinnati is attributed to increased numbers of tenants of color, social problems with unsatisfactory adjustment caused by to bad housing, and population fluxes that affect sanitation localized to the West End.

It was in this segregated market, with growing initiatives to clear slums and a city plan that came to fail wage earners who experienced housing problems, that

CMHA built Laurel Homes for white residents and Lincoln Court for black residents, segregated but side-by-side in the West End. The units were modern, but even when rented to full occupancy did not come anywhere near to equal replacement for the 750 buildings, perhaps as many as 3,000 units, lost in the buildings demolished to build them.

With immediate and continuing full occupancy of the newly built Laurel Homes and Lincoln Court, the West End remained a slum—wedged between the CBD, OTR, geographical barriers of rocky hillsides, and the commercial/industrial riverfront along the Ohio that forms the Basin. In the 1950 U.S. Census, West End population was reported as 45,358 living in 13,682 housing units. Of those units, only 1,124 were owner occupied; of the balance, there were 11,264 rental units, of which the 2,318 public housing units were but a small portion. Most of the rental units were found in deteriorating, privately held housing stock of apartment buildings and single-family homes closely situated on 25-foot × 125-foot lots with little green space. Racial segregation continued, as 72 percent of residents of the West End (32,797) were "Non-white including Negroes" (U.S. Census Bureau, 1952).

The West End fell victim to another massive slum clearance and urban renewal effort, beginning in the late 1950s, that built the major north–south I-75 interstate highway. This truncated the community, reducing both population and housing stock, but preserving Laurel Homes and Lincoln Court. Union Terminal was also spared, and the housing projects remained.

Racial segregation in housing, perpetuated by Laurel Homes and Lincoln Court, endured so that by 1990, 93 percent of the 11,352 West End residents were black, in a population density of 11,439 per square mile (geographically, the West End is less than one square mile). In the city in that year, 37.9 percent of 364,040 residents were black, living in a population density of 4,719 per square mile (Cincinnati City Council, 2004a). The dramatic reduction in population from 45,358 of the 1950 Census to 11,439 in the 1990 Census was largely related to "urban renewal" to build I-75 and to clearance of land for service roads and economic development.

Fast forward through nearly 60 years of public housing policy, and Laurel Homes and Lincoln Court had come to be defined as "severely distressed public housing," identified in the QHWRA for demolition funded through Hope VI of the late 1990s. The density of housing and enduring perceptions that the West End was a crime-infested slum, taken alongside economic development potentialities for its location between the CBD and I-75, made the West End prime target for Hope VI.

As a companion to the PRWORA (or "welfare reform"), QHWRA and funding for Hope VI provided for demolition of "severely distressed" projects like CMHA's Laurel Homes and Lincoln Court and added requirements for personal behaviors to motivate economically eligible tenants toward "self-sufficiency." It is important to note that both of these acts were dramatic policy changes in public assistance and housing subsidies, policies shifted to add requirements for client/tenant behaviors to programs that had been previously means tested. As in welfare reform aimed to reduce welfare rolls, individuals who were noncompliant with these new Hope VI provisions were to be denied assistance.

The purposes of QHWRA (hereinafter referred to as Hope VI) included policies of deregulation of public housing agencies juxtaposed with flexibility in the use of federal assistance. The act also consolidated several rental assistance programs of Section 8 of the 1937 Housing Act to favor those with more income than those previously assisted on the basis of low- or very low–income status. The purposes also include practices related to replacement communities and tenants' incomes as well as their behaviors:

> (3) facilitating mixed income communities and decreasing concentrations of poverty in public housing. . . .

> (5) creating incentives and economic opportunities for residents of dwelling units assisted by public housing agencies to work, become self-sufficient, and transition out of public housing and federally assisted dwelling units. (§ 502 PL-105-276)

Reference to replacing or revitalizing "severely distressed public housing projects" is the final purpose, as written in the act.

Cincinnati's Hope VI funding of $31 million was granted in 1998, first for Lincoln Court, with funding totaling $65 million underwritten by the Ohio Housing Finance Agency, the city of Cincinnati, and private investors. The second Hope VI grant, for Laurel Homes in 1999, totaled $90 million, with $35 million from Hope VI and $4 million from HUD's Community Express program and private investors (Local Initiatives Support Coalition, 2009). As construction began, tenants of Lincoln Court and Laurel Homes were offered rental options of relocating to other CMHA projects, remaining in units and shifting to existing units with the demolition/construction schedule, or applying for Section 8 vouchers to be taken to the open market. In theory, these options seemed workable; in practice, they had built-in problems. Prior to Hope VI, the two projects had 1,837 assisted units. On completion, there were 1,215 units, half of those available at market rate, including some restricted to home ownership, an impossibility for low-income tenants and economic others, regardless of their prior eligibility for assisted housing.

The loss of units, coupled with the transition of some to market-rate and higher income eligibility, drastically reduced units for low-income households, the very ones who are the object of "deconcentration of poverty." By 2001, when the city was consumed with the previously described Housing Impaction Ordinance, Director of Neighborhood Services Peg Moertl and Finance Director William Moller (Moller & Moertl, 2001) reported on the city's investments in Hope VI and its "reduce concentration of poverty" themes:

> Council and the Administration have supported Cincinnati Metropolitan Housing Authority's two Hope VI projects with over $15m to redevelop over 50 acres of the West End into new mixed income rental and owner-occupied housing. These two developments will demolish 1838 units on sites and replace them with 971 total units, including 250 units of ownership housing.

Research on Hope VI has presented scholars with several difficulties; each Hope VI project was different, depending on how local public housing authorities and local government used the program. In addition, as the 2004 Urban Institute research findings on Hope VI point out (Popkin et al., 2004), as the program evolved, HUD added a requirement of using local evaluators for particular programs, with no requirement that evaluation criteria include collection of data on specific performance measures. This led to a wide variation in how Hope VI was viewed. As Popkin et al. (2004) note, "in part because of the absence of definitive data and evaluation results, perceptions about the impacts of HOPE VI vary widely. Some people characterize it as a dramatic success, while others view it as a profound failure."

Regardless of these difficulties, lack of comparable data or researchable outcomes does not preclude understanding of policy implications. Should Hope VI be studied as housing policy? as deconcentration of poverty policy? as racial discrimination of public housing tenants and communities? as social policy about "hard-to-house" households in need of public assistance? or as the results in "receiving" communities as former project tenants use their vouchers? J. Fraser and Nelson's (2008) extensive study on the experience of Hope VI and mixed-income community development finds that a

> review of the literature suggests that the [Hope VI] program has been successful in improving the quality of marginalized neighborhoods (e.g. lower

crime, increased property values). Nevertheless, the program does not seem to be associated with consistently better outcomes for the original impoverished neighborhood residents it was designed to serve. (pp. 2127–2129)

In a review of the research made for the Urban Institute, Popkin et al. (2004) find that "evidence strongly supports continuation of the Hope VI approach" for its substantial successes (it demolished the most distressed and destructive housing environments, replacing it with higher quality and mixed-income housing) yet caution that if Hope VI is to continue, it needs reforms that would bring strengthened assistance with relocation and ongoing supportive services and "new attention to innovations such as 'enhanced vouchers' that would provide long-term counseling and support to vulnerable families in conjunction with housing assistance." In short, this review of many Hope VI projects cites success with buildings and deconcentration of poverty, but not with vulnerable families. Further, the remedy for Hope VI seems to focus on services for those displaced by demolition of housing projects, many of whom have been lost and are now closed out of replacement units.

Writing of the Nashville, Tennessee, experience with Hope VI, Hanna Rosin (2008) cites the work of criminologist Richard Janikowski and housing researcher Phyllis Betts, who have matched the dispersal of Section 8 voucher holders with increased crime in areas to which voucher holders moved. Their study, mapping and documenting the Nashville story, concludes that Section 8 voucher holders moving from the city to the suburbs brought increased crime to the suburbs. Their work is described, along with richly detailed anecdotal case stories, in Rosin's "American Murder Mystery" in the July/August 2008 issue of *The Atlantic*. The question and answer posed are framed as follows: "Why is crime rising in so many American cities? The answer implicates one of the most celebrated antipoverty programs of recent decades" (Rosin, 2008, p. 40). Although no one is making the claim that the Hope VI removal of distressed public housing projects or the availability of Section 8 vouchers used to deconcentrate poverty is the single factor in rising crime, Rosin (2008) reports that "researchers around the country are seeing the same basic patterns: projects coming down in inner cities, and crime pushing outward, in many cases destabilizing cities or their surrounding areas" (p. 50). (Although this report makes no claim to being scholarly research, it is well documented and appears in a respected publication.)

Allowing for the difficulty of evaluation for an ever-changing, evolving HUD program, research and evaluation of Hope VI has followed several lines of investigation, such as housing the "hard-to-house"; antipoverty policy; use of housing vouchers to disperse economically eligible tenants from housing projects to private dwellings; development of mixed-income communities; and, as in the case of Nashville, the connections between dispersal by voucher and increases in crime. Some studies place these issues in a larger context, like Goetz's (2003) studies on Minneapolis in the context of planning, redevelopment, and suburban growth and J. Fraser and Nelson's (2008) focus on resident participation in mixed-income communities and community empowerment. In much of this research, however, focus lies on the poverty of residents in crime-ridden, impoverished communities that breed social pathologies attributed to concentrations of poverty. Recommendations emanating from the research similarly focus on the residents, especially the socioeconomic factors of self-sufficiency promulgated by QHWRA. Some include recommendations for post–Hope VI enhanced vouchers and ongoing counseling. Again, the focus of both the problems and the remedy is to fix economic others, not the policies that reduce housing options for them.

In the case of Cincinnati's Hope VI, an alternative object of study emerges. The lens through which to view Hope VI is not one of demolition of distressed public housing projects for purposes of renovating housing stock, development of mixed-income communities, or the well-being of those housed at Laurel Homes and Lincoln Court. The policies and implementation plan were about involuntary deconcentration of some people for the economic development purposes of others. The policies were used to clear economic others from places coveted for economic development. The way to do it overtly was the removal of buildings that were obsolete in terms of modern building standards and, covertly, to use of the provisions of QHWRA to demolish a neighborhood for private market purposes. Researching only the impact of Hope VI on the residents without equivalent attention to market purposes distorts what happened to Laurel Homes and Lincoln Court, especially to those economic others whose housing was destroyed in the name of market economies.

As public policy to deconcentrate poverty and to promote self-sufficiency of low-income residents, Cincinnati's Hope VI had some successes; some housing project residents were "redistributed" to other projects or neighborhoods. As building demolition, Hope VI was successful; the obsolete buildings are gone, replaced by newly constructed units. As an antipoverty policy, Hope VI redistributed some households that were poor but did little more than use the policies of QHWRA to require self-sufficiency as a condition for continued housing assistance, hardly a policy to reduce poverty. Further, as an antipoverty policy, Hope VI resulted in some low-income households being lost, whether because they were unable to "fit" relocation options, were closed out of units as demolitions proceeded, or were economically unqualified to return to newly built units (the actual loss totaled nearly 1,200 units without 1:1 replacement by combination of new units and vouchers). Viewed as a policy-driven mechanism for economic development, Hope VI was successful. Even though there were requirements for mixed-income inclusion in housing developments promulgated by the private sector, places previously housing economic others ultimately included home ownership and higher levels of economic eligibility than did the projects, closing economic others out of the market.

The Local Initiatives Support Corporation (2009) evaluation of Cincinnati's Hope VI (2009) references the methodology of mixed-income neighborhoods as an attempt to restore low-income neighborhoods:

> The mixed-income community concept is a relatively new method of attempting to restore low-income communities. The success and vitality of these communities will need to be monitored for effectiveness and improvement in the lives of the residents who live there.

Like the others, this evaluation defines outcomes and effectiveness exclusively through change in the lives of residents—presumably only those who remain, not those lost to demolition and redevelopment. Missing from this view is reference to the other side of the equation, the market interests that promoted the notion that Hope VI was intended to "restore" low-income neighborhoods when, in fact, restoration was of only market-rate housing.

Richard Wright's description of urban housing realities of the 1940s resonates with Cincinnati's Hope VI experience some 60 years later. A contemporary paraphrase of Wright's words might read as follows:

> Our defenseless eyes cloud with bewilderment when we learn that there are not enough houses for us to live in. Our old projects are gone, and competing with us for new rental units are people with money who have come from the suburbs . . . the tenements we lived in were old, but they were our homes . . . new homes have signs THIS PROPERTY FOR SALE. We were told to move to make way for new "mixed income" houses that our "mix" could never afford.

"There are not enough houses for us to live in. Any day we can be told to move, that our home is to be torn down to make way for . . ."

Chapter 10

"This Little Pig Went to Market . . . this Little Pig Got None": Section 8 and Housing Choice Vouchers

This little pig went to market;
This little pig stayed at home;
This little pig had roast beef;
This little pig had none;
This little pig cried, Wee, wee, wee!
All the way home.

—Mother Goose

In an unusual convergence of federal and local housing policies enacted between 1998 and 2001, the OTR neighborhood experienced a double-whammy on community-based efforts to preserve and develop affordable housing. In 2001, the Housing Impaction Ordinance (described in chapter 8) prevented use of city-controlled housing assistance funds in neighborhoods "impacted by poverty." That local policy was coincident with implementation of new HUD policies pertaining to project-based assisted multifamily properties that had been enacted in 1998. These new federal policies dramatically changed relationships between HUD and landlords who held HUD mortgages on multifamily properties, some with housing assistance in several programs, including the Section 8 program. Some of the older mortgages had been financed by HUD's Below Market Interest Rate programs and were approaching term and refinancing; others with newer mortgages had been developed with Section 8 assistance for income-eligible tenants. The former brought down interest rates to as low as 1 percent to 3 percent, with reduced costs passed on as lower rents; the latter provided rent subsidies to fill the gap between what low-income households could pay (30 percent of income) and the established market rate for units in the multifamily buildings (for a more detailed description and evaluation of these policies, see Econometrica, Inc. & Abt Associates, Inc., 2006).

These policy shifts made by HUD began with the QHWRA with regulations on public housing and housing agency–administered programs that provided landlords with several financing or refinancing choices, popularly called "opt out," "opt in," "mark to market," and "mark up to market." The details of these programs are beyond the scope of this study; however, they served to initiate the loss of more than 1,000 units of assisted housing held by one owner in OTR, in eventualities coincident with the city's Housing Impaction Ordinance.

At the time, the OTR landlord holding substantial HUD assisted properties was Tom Denhart, who—with more than two dozen real estate partnerships—owned 201 properties with 1,089 apartment units. Since the late 1960s, Denhart's properties had been financed through HUD mortgages, most supported by Section 8 project-based assistance (Monk, 2001). Under the new opt-out and mark to market provisions, Denhart's properties were offered refinancing and a shift to tenant-based assistance. Without project-based vouchers, many units were vacated, with the option that they could be rented at market rates. Denhart's income-eligible tenants were provided with portable Section 8 vouchers that gave them a rental subsidy based on their household income, not the previous project-based assistance. Many tenants left, and new voucher holders were not attracted to the units, nor did the units attract market-rate rental tenants. Soon the buildings were closed for lack of full-rent-paying tenants, with or without assistance. Without rent-paying tenants, and unable to sell most of the buildings, even though he pursued potential for-profit and nonprofit buyers, Denhart filed for bankruptcy in August 2001, leaving now-vacant, boarded-up buildings strewn throughout OTR, doomed to be sold by the bankruptcy court and returned to the market, ripe for development.

In an interview with the *Cincinnati Enquirer* at the time of filing bankruptcy, Denhart affirmed the position taken by the *Enquirer* that it had been the policy of the city to place poverty housing nearly exclusively in one community: OTR. "It hasn't worked. It's made Over-the-Rhine the drug capital of the area. But this [low-income housing] is the business we're in. We went where the city wanted us to go" (Peale & Alltucker, 2001). Affirming the idea that the federal government, in concordance with city policy, had spent millions of dollars "making OTR a poverty reservation in the 1960s and 1970s," OTR developer and then-president of the OTR Chamber of Commerce, Chris Frutkin, called the properties owned by Denhart "the biggest impediment to market-rate housing and other projects that might bring new investment into the neighborhood" (Peale & Alltucker, 2001). Frutkin reflected the notion held by developers and some elected officials that OTR would now be ready for long-awaited upscale development. City Council member Jim Tarbell heralded the demise of Denhart's low-income housing as an opportunity to gentrify the neighborhood. Tarbell told the *Cincinnati Business Courier*, "What should have happened decades ago is going to happen now" (Monk, 2001, para. 3). Similarly, the *Courier* championed "epic changes . . . afoot in Cincinnati's most historic neighborhood" (Monk, 2001, para. 1) in a news article titled "Over-the Rhine's Future Is Now."

Community residents were caught in a policy crossfire between changing city and federal policies, bringing loss of previous public support for affordable housing development, and dramatic shifts to support for upscale development that required the claiming of buildings that once housed those who are poor and economic others. As resident and ReStoc board member Bonnie Neumeier said, "It's changing because the forces that have wanted to see Over-the-Rhine as a gold mine are here. And they are getting more support" (Monk, 2001, para. 5).

At the time of Denhart's opting out and the Section 8 changes from project-based to tenant-based assistance, the city's Planning Department was completing a two-year effort to make a *Comprehensive Plan* for OTR. Unlike several previous failed attempts, this was a major undertaking that included a wide range of stakeholders with quite disparate opinions. The working group of residents, developers, preservationists, nonprofit development corporations, real estate interests, and institutional representatives was skillfully held together by Planning Director Liz Blume, who was able to bring consensus to divisive issues that had plagued OTR for decades. The emerging plan, which was finally adopted on June 26, 2002, was titled the *Over-the-Rhine Comprehensive Plan: A Consensus-based Plan by People Who Care* (City of Cincinnati, City Planning Commission, 2002b). Goal 1 of the plan was "encourage and welcome new investments at all levels of the housing market and ensure the long-term sustainability of enough affordable housing to house current residents."

To accomplish this, the plan called for mixed-income housing, minimal displacement of low-income households, and 15- to 20-year projections of a mix of two levels of market-rate and two levels of affordable housing. Work on the plan was informed by the reality of the Housing Impaction Ordinance and the impending Denhart bankruptcy, but it offered reasonable housing goals in general, planning for 20 percent of housing at market rate, 20 percent at incomes 61 percent or more of area median income (AMI), 20 percent at 31 percent or more of AMI, and 40 percent at up to 30 percent of AMI (people at the latter level would have been eligible for Denhart's units).

Implementation of the *Over-the-Rhine Comprehensive Plan* included the following actions:

+ Create an umbrella CDC to initiate and oversee the plan implementation (established with a board and staff, board membership to include OTR resident and development community, cultural, business and financial institutions and foundations);
+ establish a TIF district (or districts) as a long-term targeted funding mechanism;
+ package financing tools (city, county, and Cincinnati Development Fund);
+ support school planning and construction activities; and
+ create a housing trust fund.

In addition to housing, the plan also included provisions for economic development, safety, transportation, and quality of life (services, cultural institutions, parks, schools, public assets). The plan was endorsed by the OTR Community Council and the several diverse working groups that had labored to bring it to consensus; it was accepted by the City Council in June 2002 as one of several neighborhood plans for the city. It became part of the larger *City of Cincinnati Comprehensive Plan*, intended to guide the city's decision making, neighborhood by neighborhood, which was managed by the Planning Department. By January 2003, the Planning Department had been abolished. The *Over-the-Rhine Comprehensive Plan* lost its administrative champion, sacrificed to dramatically changed city policy. The OTR community lost its only resource for ensuring compliance with the plan and, most important, its only recourse for grievance regarding planning and housing decisions made by the city. Soon to follow was the empowerment of the proposed CDC as 3CDC in a radically different structure than had been proposed and accepted in the plan.

The combination of the Housing Impaction Ordinance, the HUD mortgage and Section 8 voucher changes, and the community's loss of the ReStoc Vine Street Community Project, stifled efforts of OTR's nonprofit housing development corporations. At this critical juncture of policy concurrence, preserving affordable housing seemed impossible, as building of new or renovation of existing units was now impossible, legislatively prevented by federal and local policy changes. The hope for community participation in the CDC envisioned in the *Over-the-Rhine Comprehensive Plan* was soon dashed when the city turned over planning and development for OTR, downtown, and the banks to the newly formed 3CDC. Although the vision in the plan had been for a CDC with resident and community representation on its board, the 3CDC board was organized and incorporated as a nonprofit corporation with an exclusively corporate Board, most members CEOs of the city's most powerful Fortune 500 corporations.

With the community shut out, 3CDC controlled planning, development, and housing decision making and organized and gained control of TIFs and other funding resources, including the city's. By July 2003, when 3CDC began staffed operations, the population of OTR was at a 100-year low, having fallen below 7,500. Hundreds of buildings were vacant and boarded up, neighborhood schools were being consolidated for lack of enrollment, many people who were poor had moved away, and economic others had mostly vanished—except for those using shelters, soup kitchens, and social services and/or sleeping in abandoned buildings or public spaces and lingering in the park by day.

These publicly supported policy shifts, coupled with shelving of the *Over-the-Rhine Comprehensive Plan* and the demise of the city's Planning Department, shifted most housing options to an eerie combination of market-rate housing and vacant, boarded-up apartment buildings. Many low-income residents had been removed by elimination of affordable or assisted housing. People who were poor but were able to maintain long-term residency with the assistance of the neighborhood's nonprofit corporations, those few who could maintain tenancy with the few remaining private landlords, and some economic others remained in OTR, but they no longer had a voice in decision making. The Planning Department was gone, shifting city decisions to departments with virtually no grievance procedures regarding planning, development, or housing decisions. The security of HUD-assisted housing with proven leasing policies and procedures, and landlords held to building and safety standards, was gone. The decaying, boarded-up buildings had become symbolic ghosts of those who had previously called OTR their home.

At this juncture, OTR geography and its housing stock had became a developer's dream: historic Italianate architecture in a neighborhood with the majestic Music Hall; a central public park with the iconic name Washington Park, complete with an Old World bandstand and a public deep-water swimming pool; plans for a new building for the acclaimed public SCPA; and a huge housing stock, soon to be sold at bankruptcy court. As those properties were privately held, the city did not need powers of eminent domain to secure them for private development, nor was there the political will to secure them for public purposes. However, with the prospect of a bankruptcy sale, eminent domain powers were not needed as the newly formed 3CDC and its subsidiaries could "buy low" and "develop high," another instance, like the effect of the Housing Impaction Ordinance, of de facto eminent domain.

In a subsequent variation of affordable housing loss made possible by HUD opt-out policies, 230 units of assisted housing for single adults were removed from the market in nearby downtown. In 2009, tenants of the Metropole Apartments were notified that the property was being sold, and their landlord, Showe Management Corporation of Columbus, had notified HUD of intent to opt out of the HUD-financed mortgage. This sale included the rental contract for the 230 subsidized units in the building. 3CDC purchased the building and the rental contract, with a plan to redevelop the structure as a boutique hotel. Located in a prime spot—609 Walnut Street, in the artsy Backstage district of downtown— the Metropole Apartments are directly across the street from the Aronoff Center for the Arts, a complex of theatres and galleries designed by noted architect Cesar Pelli with the capacity to present Broadway shows as well as host smaller repertory and studio theatrical productions. The Metropole, once a hotel, has housed adults whose incomes qualified for HUD (initially Section 8) rental assistance for nearly 30 of its 97 years in the present location. Over the life of the HUD mortgage, tenants have all qualified for housing assistance as a result of their low incomes; many were also elderly and/or disabled. Under the terms of the HUD mortgage, the new owner, 3CDC, became responsible for implementing a plan for tenants to be relocated within one year.

The sale and the relocation of tenants were made in the name of economic development of the downtown area. As noted by the *Cincinnati Enquirer,* "Since leading a $45 million renovation of Fountain Square, the nonprofit private developer [3CDC] has set its sights on reenergizing surrounding downtown real estate and beefing up the Backstage district" (Bernard-Kuhn, 2009a, p. A16). The identified developer and operator of the planned boutique hotel is 21c Museum Hotels, whose plans are to convert the building into a 160-room hotel and "contemporary art venue." To do so, funding is being provided by the city of Cincinnati: *public* funding for *private* development, facilitated by the private corporation 3CDC. The city declared the Metropole blighted and entered into a "development and loan agreement" with 21c Museum Hotels for $4,600,000 to finance construction and development, with an additional development grant of $2,500,000 in city funds. The funding arrangements also include a Service Agreement between the City and the Developer where the Developer will pay semi-annual payments to the City equal to the amount of real property taxes that would have been paid, had an exemption not been applied to the property as allowed under Chapter 725 of the Ohio Revised Code. The City will use the payments from the Developer to pay debt service on bonds issued to finance the loan. (Dohoney, 2010)

This funding agreement was approved by City Council on March 3, 2010 (Cincinnati City Council, 2010c).

Although the agreements and funding provided by the city were seen as advancing economic development and reenergizing real estate in the downtown area, the removal of 230 assisted housing units from the district destroyed its racial, economic, and age diversity. The downtown district had been found to be one of 13 of 122 neighborhoods in Hamilton County with stable racial and economic integration since 1970. Using data on integration, socioeconomic trends, dissimilarity indices, and four U.S. Censuses beginning with 1970, the "Stable Integrated Communities Report, 2007," prepared by Brendon Wiers (2007) for the Cincinnatus Association, measured integration of 122 neighborhoods in Hamilton County (including the city of Cincinnati). The report found the downtown neighborhood to be one of "13 communities that simultaneously met diversity (between 10% and 60% black) and dispersal (blacks living on different blocks) criteria in three or more of the last four censuses" (pp. 5, 18). Downtown has a relatively small residential population. Of the 1,512 households in the 2000 U.S. Census, almost all were singles or childless, but 18 were families, and 17 percent (257 households) had incomes below poverty level (Cincinnati City Council, 2004a).

The terms of HUD financing pertaining to this sale required the purchasers to develop a relocation plan for the tenants that was HUD approved, with the understanding that the project's rent subsidies would follow eligible tenants to subsidized units of other landlords. In the case of the Metropole Apartments, the plan developed by 3CDC turned over relocation of tenants to the Model Group, a private real estate development and management company and owner of several HUD-subsidized properties. In most opt-out situations, the HUD-approved plan would have required relocation of the units to one building and compliance with all fair housing regulations. However, in this instance, the Model Group had previously received a waiver from the "project" rule. The relocation plan included offering tenants units in Model Group–owned buildings, none of which were in the downtown neighborhood.

Within 90 days of the sale, the Legal Aid Society filed a complaint with HUD about the sale and the relocation plan to disperse tenants to many buildings, none in the downtown area. The complaint was denied. In August 2010, the tenants filed a lawsuit in federal district court alleging that HUD, the city of Cincinnati, and 3CDC were in violation of fair housing laws with the Metropole relocation plan. Attorney Terence Brennen, representing the tenants, said of the lawsuit,

> It's an especially egregious violation of fair housing laws. These people shouldn't be relocated . . . the Metropole is the last significant source of low-income housing in downtown Cincinnati and its loss will force tenants to move to neighborhoods already struggling with poverty and segregation. The conversion of the Metropole is part of an effort by city officials and 3CDC, a nonprofit developer, to "systematically dismantle" housing for the poor in downtown Cincinnati. (Horn, 2010)

The sale of the Metropole Apartments for conversion into a boutique hotel is especially painful in a neighborhood that has remained stably integrated for 40 years during decades of development and redevelopment projects.

Resolution of this case came in September 2011 in an unprecedented settlement requiring 3CDC to pay the tenants $80,000, the largest such award in Cincinnati's history of relocation of tenants but a pittance proportionate to their loss. This victory for the 140 relocated tenants who remained in the case also requires 3CDC and Model Management to meet quarterly with the tenants' association, the Greater Cincinnati Coalition for the Homeless, and other affordable housing advocates to reveal their development plans and the impact on affordable housing. With this settlement, the court has affirmed the tenants' rights to their homes, and this has potential to draw 3CDC's future actions from the shadows into public light.

PART IV

The City and Econocide: Privatization of City Governance— Ensuring Economic Homogeneity

Cincinnati's long-held reputation as a managerial city, earned in the early years of the 20th century in an era of progressive reforms, shifted to that of being an *entrepreneurial* city in the century's final years. The city is governed by charter, with a nine-member City Council elected at large; a Council-hired nonpartisan city manager; and, in recent years, an independently elected mayor. Once lauded as the home of city planning (Knack, 1980) and a progressive, nonpartisan form of municipal governance (Gerckens, 1980), Cincinnati's managerial structure entailed the city manager being responsible for planning and economic development. This lasted until 2002, when the city's 80-year-old Planning Department was dissolved. This abrupt decision was prompted by denial of permits for a "big box" store development in a residential neighborhood. But a few months later, in 2003, city functions of planning, development, zoning, housing, and social service decisions and implementation were shifted to newly organized public–private partnerships.

The overriding goals of this new form of governance were driven by city government and business interests vigorously promoting "business success," as prominently stated at the top of the city's Web site home page (http://www.cincinnati.oh.us/):

Nestled among the hills of the Ohio River Valley, the City of Cincinnati has the personality and charm of an Old World city, complemented by the stature of a world class business center. With a generous share of Fortune

500 companies and a diverse roster of solid small, mid-sized, and larger businesses in its boundaries, Cincinnati offers virtually everything needed for business success. That includes the resources so vital to a globally aware community, solid and comfortable neighborhoods, strong families, and well-rounded individuals.

In practice, business-oriented success is manifest in zealous adherence to promotion of an economically homogenous community in which business/profit/market interests predominate and economic others are in constant jeopardy of removal. In the case of Cincinnati, promotion of economic homogeneity, under the imprimatur of government, required the formation of new private entities empowered to effectuate public as well as private decision making. Underlying these notions skewed to promote economic homogeneity, three political maneuvers predominate, orchestrated and implemented in lockstep by business interests and city government:

+ Government/governance cedes functions of economic development, planning, zoning, housing, and decision making on expenditures and allocations of public resources to public–private partnerships and contracts long-term management of public assets—such as the public square, parks, parking garages, and recreational facilities—to subsidiaries of public–private partnerships;

+ mechanisms/legislation are sanctioned and implemented by government for removal of populations and social services deemed to interfere with economic homogeneity, including removal of economic others (especially those whose circumstances and behaviors are deemed counter to notions of an economically homogenous community); and

+ government/governance is extended to include mandated models for location and delivery of social services with "best practices" emanating from business/entrepreneurial principles rather than expertise of professional disciplines of and research in social work, psychology, mental health/substance abuse, or medicine, with mandated models implemented through outsourced decision making on allocation of the city's funds for human services, vindictive public funding decisions on use of federal funds for assisted housing and social and treatment services, and implementation of restrictive zoning codes and operational standards.

Examples of policies and the above-named shifts in governance to privatization considered here are the following:

+ dissolution of the city's Planning Department (2002);
+ establishment and empowerment of 3CDC, incorporating DCI (2003);
+ City Council Resolution (No. 41-2008) to revise city zoning code to reduce and restrict "concentration of social services in areas deemed impacted" (2008);
+ recommendation of 32 zoning text amendments to the code restricting zones to "reduce the concentration of social services" (2009);
+ Homeless Services Ordinance (No. 347-2008), mandating development of a plan for sheltering homeless single adults to prevent "behaviors that are disruptive to business and residents" and that shelter facilities become "good neighbors" (2008); and
+ Policy-driven removal/relocation of the DIC shelter for single homeless people (2008).

These shifts to privatization of city governance move most decision-making processes from the public to private sector and facilitate relentless, policy-driven removal of economic others in the contemporary phenomenon of econocide— a collectivity of victims disappears, removed from the market *and*, thereby, the community, sanctioned by a collectivity of the privileged with a goal of economic homogeneity.

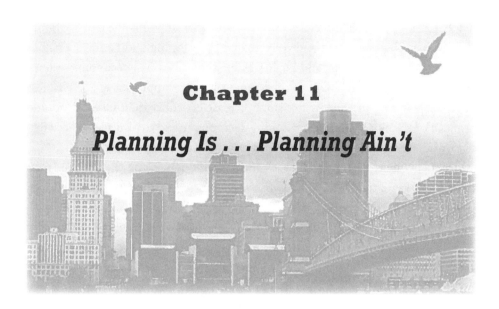

Chapter 11

Planning Is . . . Planning Ain't

This is the Official City Plan of the City of Cincinnati. The result of the labor of many hands, of years of collection and study of data and of constant and painstaking consideration and revision, it is presented to the citizens of Cincinnati as an earnest, sincere attempt to plan for the orderly development of the city during the fifty years to come. . . . This City Plan and Program, the first officially adopted by any city in the United States of the size of Cincinnati or larger, is now the law of the city.

—*Official City Plan of Cincinnati, Ohio* (1925)

Cincinnati Planning Department Abolished at Behest of Big Box Developer

—Headline, April 1, 2003, *The New Rules Project Newsletter,*
Institute for Local Self-reliance

Legislation and administration of public policy in cities, especially as related to housing and economic development, have been shaped by planning and zoning theory and practice since the turn of the 20th century. The account of municipal planning that follows here traces the 78-year evolution of planning in Cincinnati, regarded as a pioneer in urban planning, dating from reform movements of the 1920s. Although it is an account of planning policy and practices, it also traces the critical balance between neighborhood and business interests. It is in that balancing that economic others, along with their low-income neighbors, are affected by policies enacted and perpetuated by planning and zoning decisions made by both government and business. For some, especially economic others, planning decisions contribute to their removal and disappearance. For business interests, planning and zoning decisions increase or reduce their investments and profits. For the city, planning and zoning decisions attend to or neglect social justice through the balancing of public and private interests and obligations.

The Cincinnati Planning Department, long thought to be the first and best of its kind, came to a sudden end with the adoption of the city's 2003 budget, and with it came the abdication of public responsibility for the city's *Comprehensive Plan* and dozens of neighborhood plans developed within the community. Although the Planning Department was eliminated in the name of closing a budget deficit of $35 million and reducing government to focus on basic services, the act shifted responsibility for planning from being a public to a private function. The much-lauded planning director, Elizabeth Blume, left at year's end, the Planning Commission cried "foul." The balance of the story is that a powerful member of the city's appointed Economic Development Task Force, who disagreed with the Planning Department's denial of approval for his plan to build a shopping center of big box stores in a residential neighborhood, pressured the city to abolish the Planning Department. The Economic Task Force was co-chaired by business and government leaders: the president of the Fifth Third Bank and the city manager. The developer's shopping center proposal conflicted with the neighborhood's plan and, hence, was not approved by the Planning Department. Rather than address the matter by established grievance and appeal procedures, the mayor and the city manager, yielding to pressure from the developer, found budgetary reasons to dismantle the 78-years-old Planning Department. The big-box development proceeded.

The Official City Plan of Cincinnati, Ohio (1925)

One irony of the abolition of the Planning Department, vigorously driven by influential business interests, is that the department had arisen from just such influence on city government in the 1920s. The history of the Cincinnati Planning Department begins in municipal reforms of the Progressive Era, at a time when Cincinnati was bankrupted by corrupt politicians and ward bosses who had received millions of dollars in graft for never-completed capital construction and public utility franchises. At the time, the city had "one of the highest tax rates for the level of public services in America" (Gerckens, 2001). Reforms leading to the first adopted comprehensive city plan began with the successful campaign of charter reform activists for a new city charter in 1924. The new charter provided for the election of a nine-member City Council that was seated in 1925. The newly elected City Council appointed a mayor from its own ranks, hired a politically neutral city manager, and established a civil service system for hiring city workers. The newly formed charter government adopted *The Official City Plan of Cincinnati, Ohio, Adopted by the City Planning Commission, 1925,* which claimed to be "the first officially adopted by any city in the United States of the size of Cincinnati or larger, [and] is now the law of the city" (City of Cincinnati Planning Commission, 1925, p. 1).

The *Plan* was comprehensive, addressing and codifying by ordinance civic matters of land use, zoning, transit, community development, subdivisions and housing, parks and playfields, streets, and garbage and refuse disposal. It addressed both zoning and public investment in capital projects; it also established a Citizens' City Planning Committee (later to become the Planning Commission) with a citizen majority membership. Historian David Stradling notes that these reforms brought positive changes in efficiency in government as well as stabilization of the city's debt. "Almost overnight the city's reputation turned 180 degrees, from among the worst run cities in the nation to among the best" (Stradling, 2003, p. 96).

The Official City Plan of Cincinnati, Ohio (City of Cincinnati Planning Commission, 1925) was researched and authored by lawyer Alfred Bettman, along with the volunteer United City Planning Committee, which he organized. Bettman, formerly the city solicitor, later served as planning consultant to both the Hoover and Roosevelt administrations. In addition, he had drafted the legislation enacted by the Ohio legislature (in 1915) that paved the way for the establishment of unpaid municipal planning commissions in Ohio municipalities. Without the state legislation, the city planning commission would have had no authority. Bettman also authored the winning brief in the precedent-setting zoning case *Euclid, Ohio v. Ambler Realty Co.* (1926), argued before the Supreme Court, which upheld earlier decisions affirming municipal zoning power.

Planning commissions with a citizens' majority were included as one element of Bettman's notions of reform of municipal government, so by the time the reformers brought charter reform to Cincinnati, there was a city plan ready for adoption and a planning commission in place. Within the new council–city manager form of government, a Planning Department staffed by professionals under the leadership of Bettman's colleague Ladislas Segoe was established.

The *Plan* of 1925 boldly claimed to be a plan for 50 years, drawn from the latest data on existing conditions and future projections. It addressed growth and development needs through use of statistical data on population trends; scientific data on topography, geological formations, waterways, and utilities; and social science theory related to civic purposes such as schools, parks, public buildings, public transportation, and health and sanitation. Each of the 18 articles of the *Plan* provided direction on zoning and location of buildings for specific purposes such as public services, garbage disposal, transportation venues, schools, and residential housing. Projections were made on both public and private new development (geographically, the city was not built-out in 1925) and on redevelopment needs of various populations of the city.

The *Plan* is silent on the needs of people who are poor, with the exception of the article titled "Subdivisions and Housing" (pp. 39–54). Like the other articles, "Subdivisions and Housing" begins with the ordinance providing platting law and platting and land use rules and regulations. However, unlike the other articles, it frames the plan in problem-based terminology in a section titled "Housing Problems in Cincinnati." With citation of a study by the Housing Betterment League of Cincinnati, the problem is initially described as one of few vacancies, overcrowding, and constantly escalating tenement rents. In fact, the problem is so bad, with influx of population in the Great Migration, with "nearly 3,500 new colored people since 1920" (pp. 50–51) that 10 percent of all dwellings in the city are tenements, 30 percent of the total population lives in tenements, and 80 percent of the tenements are in the Basin: OTR and the West End. The Basin, the *Plan* continues, is also where

> the majority of the colored people live . . . in the West End most of the oldest and more unsanitary tenements are occupied by colored people, where they often live six, seven, eight and even twelve people in a single room. These slum conditions could be much improved if the City had available even normal means for their control. (p. 50)

The *Plan* does not suggest what those "means for their control" might be but proposes that the solution to the housing problem is the construction of new houses at a cost of $5,000, including the land, requiring $600 annual rent "to produce a safe investment." The *Plan* continues: "It is therefore obvious that the construction of single-family homes can not meet the needs of the mass of the colored population and the white low-wage earners" (p. 51). Housing mobility is projected in the *Plan* as those in better circumstances moving to newly constructed housing that are beyond the means of "colored people and white low wage-earners" (p. 51) and newly vacant tenements becoming available to those who can afford them. The final conclusion offered by the *Plan* to address the housing problem is this:

> This means that it is not feasible now to give any consideration as a part of the City Plan to providing housing for low wage-earners, and that attention should be concentrated now on the amelioration of living conditions in the older part of the town by zoning protection and by provision of parks, playgrounds, community centers and open spaces. (p. 51)

So, no city attention is to be directed toward the housing problem of low wage-earners—blacks and poor whites—but zoning protections are to be offered to the Basin, gradually disappearing with the invasion of business and industry. Further, it is not economical to "reproduce the more objectionable features of low rent old tenements, thanks to the Zoning Ordinance and Building Code" (p. 51).

With the exception of the construction of housing for low-income families at Laurel Homes and Lincoln Court in the West End by the Public Housing Authority (described in chapter 9), this abandonment of public responsibility for affordable housing became the policy basis for the city's housing policy and future plans. The *Plan* writes off public responsibility for addressing affordable housing and, with it, consideration of social obligation inclusive of all citizens, most crucially economic others. It set in place the theoretical underpinnings of future housing and development policies, limiting policy attention to the use of public resources to develop, redevelop, or retain affordable housing. Although the *Plan* was driven by citizen effort and citizen participation, it is silent on economic others and their housing needs. They are omitted as having no place because housing for them cannot "produce a safe investment": *Planning is ... but planning ain't for everyone.*

The City's Planning Department and the *Official City Plan* of 1925 enjoy recognition by city planners throughout North America as the first and best. Born of social and political reform, planning as envisioned by Alfred Bettman, Ladislas Segoe, and other giants of municipal planning included a clear role for citizens that went beyond what might now be called "citizen or community input." Although planners employed by the city were trained professionals, the Planning Commission required a citizen majority membership, with final approval for planning decisions held by a council voted by citywide (not ward) electorate. In 1980, the American Planning Association held its annual meeting and conference in Cincinnati, thematically billing it as a location "where planning ... is considered a virtue" (Knack, 1980, p. 14). Lawrence C. Gerckens (1980), a historian of

American planning, concluded one session of the conference noting the reform history of planning as birthed in Cincinnati:

> Planning in Cincinnati has consistently been at the forefront of emerging American planning practice. Planning came to Cincinnati as citizen-generated reform and flourished as an element of urban policy, creating a model for other American cities. Not bad for the "worst-governed city." Welcome, planners to Cincinnati. Welcome home. (p. 23)

The 50-year plan was in effect for fewer than 25 years, at which point a master plan project was launched, leading to adoption of *The Cincinnati Metropolitan Master Plan and the Official City Plan* in 1948 (City of Cincinnati Planning Commission, 1948).

The Cincinnati Metropolitan Master Plan and the Official City Plan of the City of Cincinnati (Adopted November 22, 1948)

The broad objectives of the 1948 plan, commonly identified as the *Master Plan* (City of Cincinnati Planning Commission, 1948), continued themes from the 1925 plan: "The City Planning Commission has recognized promotion of the social and economic welfare of the people of the Area as the basic purpose of the Master Plan" (p. 7). The *Master Plan* continued, citing both "most satisfying and healthful living conditions" and "highest degree of economic well-being attainable by [the city's] people" (p. 7) as goals. This plan was positioned as a regional plan, inclusive of the city of Cincinnati; the other cities, villages, and townships in Hamilton County, Ohio; and municipalities across the Ohio River in northern Kentucky. And, like the 1925 *Plan*, the *Master Plan* addressed matters of land use, zoning, residential and industrial areas, public transportation, public buildings, and schools. Parks were addressed in a separate plan, prepared and adopted by the Parks Commission, that had its roots in the 1907 *Parks and Parkways Plan* (Kessler, 1907).

The *Master Plan* begins with traditional planning data pertaining to population trends, economic and employment prospects, neighborhood conditions (including "deteriorated and declining areas"), and zoning for industrial use, and it provides many maps, particularly of areas not yet developed at the time of the 1925 *Plan*. Unlike the 1925 *Plan*, the *Master Plan* made general recommendations rather than specific ones. For example, in 1925, the *Official City Plan* proposed a board of education building to be located in the vicinity of Central Parkway and Elm Street, but the *Master Plan* recommended "benefits of grouping" for locations of public buildings such as administrative services or cultural ven-uesAlthough not written as another 50-year plan, the *Master Plan* was visionary in attending to suburbanization and expansion, captured under the title "The Outward Movement." Regarding this emerging phenomenon of development at the city outskirts pushing into unincorporated and rural areas, Cincinnati is described as subsidizing such outward development in that residents of these outlying areas "enjoy many city services at the expense of the central city" (p. 8). Among the services are streets, lights, traffic control, food and building inspection, but also public library, museums, parks, airports and public institutions "available to those residing beyond the Cincinnati corporation line at little or no expense to them. . . . But there is another side to the coin" (p. 8).

The other side of the coin is what happens in the older portion of the city— namely, the inner city—now seen as ill fitted for contemporary needs. Citing depreciation of property values and deterioration and obsolescence of housing stock in the inner city, coupled with "injurious" mixed use for industrial purposes allowed prior to the 1925 *Plan*, planners saw the inner city as posing two problems: provision for orderly development of the periphery and restoration and maintenance of the livability of the inner communities. Data collected for this plan revealed that 63,000 dwelling units, or 34 precent of all housing units, were "deficient on the basis of structural condition or sanitary facilities" (p. 68). Of those deficient units, 90 percent (56,390 units) were located in the Basin and adjacent communities—the West End, OTR, and areas along the river and Mill Creek. The percentage of deficient housing units, called "tenements" in the 1925 *Plan*, had risen from 10 percent to 34 percent in 20 years. The *Master Plan* is silent on how many people lived in that 34 percent of the housing units, but it is clear that these were the populations that could not afford to move to the new housing projected in the 1925 *Plan*. Those who lived in 1948's "deficient units," having housing roots in 1925's "tenements," included each era's economic others: low-wage earners; blacks; immigrants from the south; and those displaced by, but *not* housed in, the new public housing in Laurel Homes and Lincoln Court.

The *Master Plan* does not make recommendations with as much specificity as did the earlier plan, but it recommends activities for residential areas, making a "must do" list: continuous study of local housing conditions, rehabilitation of declining areas that cannot be cleared for years, and provision of housing for low-income families displaced by redevelopment and public improvements activities. The reference to displacement of low-income families does not include families or residents but, rather, deterioration and obsolescence of housing stock. There was no plan for relocation of low-income residents when Laurel Homes and

Lincoln Court were built. And, to some interpretations, the demolition of tene-ments in the West End to build the projects resulted in a hard-to-count (due to overcrowded, subdivided flats) but significant net loss of housing units. Those lost units had housed low-wage earners, economic others who were written off by the 1925 *Plan* as not able to afford housing "that produced a safe investment." Other buildings in blighted areas were in badly deteriorated condition. The *Master Plan* recommendations for industrial development and investment in busi-ness cite the need for municipalities to have ways to clear such blighted areas for redevelopment.

Blighted areas were located in the Basin and along the riverfront, inhabited by economic others. Redevelopment, by definition in the *Master Plan*, "means com-plete demolition of buildings and restoration of the cleared land to the market under whatever controls have been adopted by the public authorities for the spec-ified area" (p. 70). Once again, policy directions adopted in the *Master Plan* gave priority to economic development over rehabilitation of housing, and regional objectives related to emerging suburbanization rather than the inner city. *Plan-ning is . . . planning ain't . . . for economic others.*

The Coordinated City Plan and the Comprehensive Land Use Plan (1980)

The officially titled *Coordinated City Plan and the Comprehensive Land Use Plan* (City of Cincinnati Planning Commission, 1980) is usually referred to as the *Comprehensive Plan of 1980*. By the time it was adopted, matters of housing and economic development in cities had changed as a result of several federal initiatives, most important the Housing and Community Development Act of 1974, which brought cities funding in CDBG programs. The 1980 *Plan* reflects advances made in planning theory since the original plan, drawing from fields of economic growth and analysis, urban and regional planning, and environmental quality. Matters of social equity had been drawn into planning and economic theory by programs of the Great Society, the War on Poverty, and Model Cities. Later, new national interests in environmental protection, energy conservation, and land use related to urban sprawl emerged and influenced urban planning (see Krueckeberg, 1994, pp. 20–27).

The *Comprehensive Plan of 1980* was framed with nine "functional elements," largely encompassing the categories from the previous plans. The elements ranged from industrial and commercial development, to public safety facilities, to utility systems, to transportation. "Residential Areas" of the 1948 *Master Plan* became

"Neighborhood Revitalization" in the 1980 *Plan*, with the goal being to "facilitate decent, adequate housing within safe, stable and pleasant neighborhoods" (p. 14). Because this plan identified strategies related to "functional elements," it promoted frameworks of assistance for neighborhood revitalization according to the degree of housing deterioration. For areas of high deterioration, the strategy was revitalization of housing stock; for areas of moderate decline, it was conservation of housing stock; and for those without deterioration, it was maintenance.

Merged into the neighborhood revitalization functional element were federal housing and neighborhood development programs, especially those eligible for funding through CDBGs. In fact, the exclusive plan for neighborhood revitalization was the CDBG plan for two of the three housing strategies, revitalization and conservation of housing stock. Conditions for revitalization were specified as "a predominance of low/moderate income populations in areas of high blight" (p. 14), whereas the conditions for conservation of housing stock were a "predominance of low/moderate income populations in areas of moderate to limited blight" (p. 14). Those strategies were planned entirely for use of federal funding sources. The final housing strategy—maintenance of housing stock—was planned for a "preponderance of moderate/high incomes in areas of little or no blight" (p. 14).

The *Comprehensive Plan of 1980* housing strategies for revitalization assign a key role to the city in property acquisition and capital improvements: "In general, revitalization strategies [for areas of high blight] involve a major public role in the redevelopment process" (p. 14). The housing conservation strategy was planned to "emphasize private expenditures for improvement *e.g.*, housing rehabilitation . . . the city's role is to promote or facilitate private expenditures, such as loan programs" (p. 14).

These revitalization and conservation housing strategies were planned for exclusive use of CDBG funds, and a list of named projects appears in the plan:

> The Plan is based on the assumption that some of the new residential land use will include federally assisted housing located in conformance with the Planning Commission's Housing Allocation Policy. That Policy is aimed at expanding housing opportunities for low and moderate income families in areas not previously available to them. The Policy conforms with the Regional Area-wide Housing Opportunity Plan for assisted housing. Public financial incentives, however should be designed to minimize displacement and should induce voluntary relocation from marginal housing. (p. 35)

The housing policy in the 1980 *Plan* shifts low-income housing from tenements (1925) or deficient housing (1948) to housing in blighted areas with a "predominance of low/moderate populations." Although it may seem a semantic shift, it does begin to connect the existence of blighted areas to the populace rather than buildings and housing stock, an issue that became critically important in later discourse on communities or neighborhoods with "concentrations of poverty."

In another shift of planning, unlike the 1925 and the 1948 *Plans*, the 1980 *Plan* did make it a matter of policy to "minimize displacement." The words of the 1925 *Plan* absolving the city of any responsibility for housing for low-wage earners and instructing it instead to "concentrate on amelioration of living conditions in older parts of town by zoning protection and provision of open spaces" (City of Cincinnati Planning Commision, 1925, p. 51) left low-income and economic other populations out of the plan. The 1948 *Plan* bridged the earlier and later plans by planning for a housing advisory authority to provide assistance to housing providers, not the low-income earners or economic others who were displaced. The 1980 *Plan* shifts housing planning and policy for low- to moderate-income households to federal funding responsibilities, taking them "off the grid" of city responsibility and freeing up public initiatives for economic and housing development driven by the market. *Planning is for market consumers . . . planning ain't for low-wage earners, no-wage earners, and economic others.*

The *Comprehensive Plan of 1980* continues, to date, as the city's official plan, along with dozens of neighborhood plans, parks and recreation plans, downtown development plans, and so on. Neighborhood plans originate with citizen input, typically forged through neighborhood councils working with city staff; they are approved by the Planning Commission and sent to the City Council for final approval. In late 2009, the city committed staff and budget to begin a communitywide process to develop the next city plan.

And Then . . . Planning Ain't

The City of Cincinnati Planning Department—staffed by professional planners, not political appointees—had been the administrative center for executing the work and responsibilities of the independent Planning Commission until the city dissolved it with the adoption of the 2003 city budget.

"Planning's gone, zeroed out," as one neighborhood activist said, "how could *that* happen?" The chairman of the Planning Commission said, "It's unfortunate if a dust-up over big-box stores in [the neighborhood of] Oakley led to this, I suspect it has a lot to do with it" (Korte, 2002a, p. 14). Another citizen member of the Planning Commission said to the *Business Courier* (Monk, 2003), "I find it very odd that [the developer] participated in making the recommendation to abolish the very department that is regulating what he's trying to do" (para. 8) and "called the mayor's development task force a 'stacked deck' that is very heavily weighted toward developer interests" (para. 9). The president of the local community council agreed. She pointed out, also reported in the *Courier*, that the developer represents the "future of the city developer-wise, and that's a very scary specter indeed" (Monk, 2003, para. 7), going on to say, "This whole thing is a sham. We feel our neighborhood is under siege by developers" (para. 10).

The American Planning Association weighed in on the elimination of the Planning Department. The Association objected, raising alarm at the abolition of an independent department. In the Association's *Planning Journal*, Osborne (2003) wrote, "The birthplace of modern urban planning is the scene of what some say is the movement's latest setback ... Cincinnati officials eliminated the city's independent planning department" (p. 36).

The city's official statement was tersely worded in the ordinance "Amending the Cincinnati Municipal Code by repealing Article XXV, Department of City Planning" of the Administrative Code (Cincinnati City Council, 2002). The independent Planning Commission countered with a unanimously adopted resolution:

> Request City Council to retain an independent planning department to serve the City Council, the Planning Commission and the neighborhoods in a professional way as it has since the adoption of the Charter as the purpose was originally envisioned and continues to be valid today, that being the balancing of neighborhood and development interests. (City of Cincinnati Planning Commission, 2002a)

With the departure of the planning director and the adoption of the 2003 budget without a Planning Department, the city manager shifted planning and zoning functions to a newly configured Department of Community Development, renaming it the Department of Community Development and Planning, "appointed by and subject to the control and supervision of the city manager" (Cincinnati City Council, 2003a). This administrative decision shifted all neighborhood services, human services, small business services, and planning services to a merged department. All functions for developers, development authorities, and development corporations promoting economic development were shifted to the Economic Development Department, also under the auspices of the city manager.

In simultaneous initiatives, policies were set in place per the directions of the Economic Development Task Force to establish private development corporations to take over functions of planning, administration of the city's development funds, and economic development for geographically specific areas of the city.

The descriptions of the 3CDC that follow are a business-driven sequel to the abolition of the Planning Department directed to economic development of and planning for Downtown, the Riverfront, and OTR. Coincident with these policy shifts, the previously described changes in HUD housing policies for opt out and HCV/Section 8 housing assistance provided a government-driven reduction, if not elimination, of low-income housing, facilitating availability of coveted buildings for private redevelopment. In both, the winners were business interests and private developers, and the losers were economic others.

Viewed through the lens of promotion of economic development and business interests, the elimination of the Planning Department was an enormous success. Viewed through a lens of social obligation and municipal governance, the elimination was a substantial reversal of established democratic processes. In many ways, it set up the potential for the kind of corruption and graft of the 1920s that prompted the formation of the original *Official City Plan of Cincinnati, Ohio* and established the Planning Commission. By most accounts, the decision to abolish the Planning Department was made to clear the way for a politically powerful developer to violate both the city's *Plan* and zoning codes after the department denied *his* plans for big box stores. Rather than follow established procedures to grieve the decision and/or develop a negotiated plan accommodating his request as well as the approved neighborhood plan, the city abolished the Planning Department. This immediately shifted the issue from a planning/zoning decision to a constitutional (charter) issue. It transferred planning authority from the city to private developers, conveying planning and zoning authority from an independent planning commission to private interests, far exceeding the controversy surrounding one development.

With the demise of the Planning Department, all entities—public, private, individual, neighborhood, civic, and business—were denied independent planning and, with it, equity in application of codes as established in a civil, democratic governance according to the City Charter. This decision did far more than accommodate one powerful, disgruntled developer. It initiated a legal way for the powerful to run roughshod over a neighborhood, violating the neighborhood's and the city's established, approved plan.

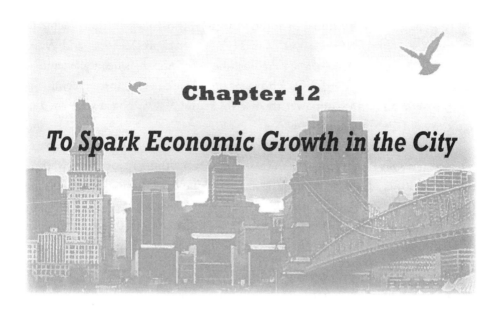

Chapter 12

To Spark Economic Growth in the City

Be it resolved that the City Manager direct a panel comprised of private sector and other leaders appointed by the Mayor to reform economic development in the City. This panel shall make recommendations to the Mayor and Council on steps the City must take to spark economic growth in the city, including consideration of, but not limited to, full-scale regulatory reforms as well as the potential creation of an independent development authority that can issue bonds and utilize eminent domain powers.

—City of Cincinnati, Resolution No. 2002-5079,
adopted April 22, 2002

An Economic Development Task Force, charged by Cincinnati City Council in 2002 to reform economic development in the city, recommended "full-scale regulatory reform" and the creation of a development authority empowered to issue bonds and "utilize eminent domain." The report of the task force was accepted by the city council on April 23, 2003, but implementation had already begun. By July 2003, 3CDC was formed according to the recommendations. As an independent, private development corporation, it was empowered to issue bonds and to use powers of eminent domain, thereby shifting those powers from the public to the private sector.

The task force had been co-chaired by the president of the Fifth Third Bank (5/3) and the city manager, with a significant majority of members drawn from the city's largest corporations. In addition to 5/3, those corporations included Procter & Gamble (P&G), Kroger, Macy's (Federated Stores), Cintas, and Western & Southern Life. All of these were Fortune 500 companies headquartered in Cincinnati, all with senior CEOs who went on to use the task force recommendations to organize and empower themselves as the 3CDC board with the full authority of City Council.

As described in chapter 11, the abolishment of the city's Planning Department, also having originated with the task force, paved the way for this privatization and shifting of the city's planning and development functions to 3CDC for the "precincts" of Fountain Square, OTR, and the Banks.

As described in the task force's report (City of Cincinnati, 2003b), the purpose of this privatization move was to create a new development corporation that

> will serve as a non-profit, privately-led corporation responsible for enhancing downtown Cincinnati's position as a regional center of high value employment, housing, as well as arts, culture and entertainment. . . . The CDC will be a non-profit, private-sector-led corporation. The Board of Directors will be a [sic] comprised 9–11 senior level CEO's from the downtown business community. The President of the CDC should be retained as a result of a national search. Staff will be senior executives with substantial experience in planning and executing large-scale public/private real estate development transactions and should be familiar with the political environment of development as well as the technical aspects of the development process.

The board was exclusively corporate—highest level leaders, with membership so narrow as to exclude representation from any other constituency or community than boardrooms of major corporations.

The first board chair of 3CDC was A. G. Lafley, then C.E.O. of P&G. His vision for the new corporation was to take the city from "good to great" ("3CDC— New Deal-Maker," 2003). The 3CDC board announced that this self-described new "deal-making group" would raise $150 million in five years, with commitment from the city of $100 million in tax increment funding, empowerment zone, and CDBG funds. The $50 million balance was to be raised through corporate contributions. The *Cincinnati Enquirer* began positioning news and editorial coverage of this new corporation as a "private corporation driven by the public-private partnership in projects that are to include new housing, shops, offices, and arts reaching from the riverfront through Over-the-Rhine" ("3CDC—New Deal-Maker," 2003, p. C6). The partnering aspects of this public–private partnership extended to the city were only for financing and funding contributions, not partnership in decision making.

The ideology of 3CDC as articulated by Lafley clearly mirrors the kinds of corporate drivers that have guided P&G's worldwide success in the global economy: "return-oriented, results-oriented, execution-oriented, making sure that investors get a good return on their investment in new development" ("3CDC— New Deal-Maker," 2003, p. C6). Subsequently, 3CDC assumed management of the newly established Cincinnati New Markets Fund, Inc., using the federal New Market Tax Credit Program and the existing Cincinnati Equity Fund, Ltd. These public–private funding partnerships function as managers of public and private financial and funding resources, with decision making entirely and exclusively surrendered to 3CDC.

The enabling legislation (Cincinnati City Council, 2003b), as well as public sentiment for this shift in governance, carried few provisions for accountability, with generalities rather than specifics on which powers and authority of the city were transferred to 3CDC. The city's public responsibilities for planning and economic development for Fountain Square, the Riverfront, and OTR, previously held by city administration, were surrendered to this privately constituted corporation by management contracts. The contracts authorized 3CDC to act for the public sector under the imprimatur of the government, without provision for accountability beyond the management contracts or for redress of grievances, ensuring, as Lafley pointed out, "a good return on investment in new development."

This shift in governance of planning, economic development, and asset management arose through several ideas converging around notions of privatization: the downsizing of government, rejection of regulatory authority held by the Planning Commission and the city's permitting authority, and reducing or eliminating the influence of public service professionals in decision making. These changes had originated in response to political pressure from the business community, long frustrated with the ways personnel in city departments handled development in areas such as downtown retail venues (Leibovitz & Salmon, 1999), Fountain Square, and the long-awaited riverfront development called "The Banks" and planned for housing in neighborhoods like OTR and for retail development in neighborhoods like Oakley.

Examination of the experience of the city of Cincinnati with changed relationships between municipal governance, private business, and the public provides ways to understand some of the impact of privatization on the larger community. Of particular interest here is the impact on economic others who, as previously described, may be easily ignored—in this instance, deliberately excluded from the market as well as decision making in the civic domain and vulnerable to exclusion or removal from certain areas of the city.

Beginning in mid-2003, 3CDC engaged in planning and development activities in three areas that affect the entire community and require scrutiny regarding public purpose and disclosure: public asset management, privatization of city planning and economic development, and use of de facto eminent domain to acquire land.

Asset Management of Fountain Square

Fountain Square, at the center of the city's downtown area, is best known for the Tyler Davidson Fountain, an ornamental bronze water fountain with the figure "Genius of the Water" rising nearly 50 feet above the plaza. As described in the 1943 *WPA Guide to Cincinnati*, Fountain Square was seen as the cultural and commercial center of the City: "Fountain Square is the heart of the City—a sentimental nosegay—the core of the City's civic, social, and commercial life" (WPA, 1943/1987, pp. 179–180). Governor Rutherford B. Hayes spoke at the dedication of the fountain in 1871, six years before he was elected president. Fountain Square has since hosted the frenzied celebration of the Armistice on November 11, 1918, and has been the site of dozens of presidential campaign rallies and wild celebrations in the years the Cincinnati Reds won the World Series. It provides the venue for events of many civic groups, and cultural events from Oktoberfest Zinzinnati (reputedly the largest Octoberfest outside Munich), to Horticultural Society displays, to memorials for victims of domestic violence, and it is *the* place for public expression and free speech on contentious issues. Fountain Square history also includes several legally contested attempts at permitted (or denied) public expression of controversial opinions (for example, Menorahs, Christmas Nativity scenes, Ku Klux Klan crosses), antiwar demonstrations, and removal of panhandlers. That the iconic fountain and Fountain Square are public assets is unquestionable—owned by the city, dedicated to public use, and perhaps singularly the city's public venue.

In 2003, when the city announced the initiation of 3CDC, Fountain Square was specifically included in what was surrendered to the new public–private partnership. The city gave 3CDC the authority to "oversee the City's Plan projects and programs to strengthen and leverage downtown's core assets, initially focusing on Fountain Square, Over-the-Rhine and the Banks" (City of Cincinnati, 2003a). Soon, 3CDC had a contract with the city that surrendered full planning, development, and management authority for Fountain Square for 50 years, initially exempting the authority to issue use permits for the square. By 2006, that authority was also handed over to 3CDC. The city's initial reluctance to surrender authority for issuance of permits for use of Fountain Square was related to a troubled history of issuing or denying permits for religious symbols and hate speech, some settled by the courts.

In the transmittal to City Council of the ordinance to transfer permitting functions to 3CDC, the city manager wrote,

> Passage of ordinance will retain the past availability of Fountain Square for public purposes while also allowing the day to day managers of Fountain Square better opportunity to maximize the use of the facility for activities that are intended to attract more visitors to Fountain Square. (Rager, 2006)

The wording of this ordinance heralded new usages for Fountain Square, promoting activities more "theme park" than "free speech."

Soon to follow was a contract for the planning and redevelopment of Fountain Square and the Fountain Square parking garage. The language of the enabling ordinance was clear: "to provide all development management services in connection with the redevelopment of the property" and "to provide all management services that may be required by the City of Cincinnati in connection with the day-to-day operation of Fountain Square Plaza" (Cincinnati City Council, 2005). With this ordinance, authority for planning, development, and issuance of permits for public space, functions of the public sphere, and decisions about this public space and assets no longer resided with government but with a private development corporation by management contract.

Beginning in 2007, 3CDC completed what became a $48 million redesign, redevelopment, and reconstruction of Fountain Square infrastructure, using $4 million in public funds and $44 million in private investments (Zeleznik, 2010). Concurrent with the development of the public space and underground parking garage at Fountain Square, private real estate and business investments totaling $53 million were to pay for major building improvements, new retail business, upscale housing with condominiums and lofts, and restaurants (Cincinnati Center City Development Corporation, 2010a).

Simultaneous with the real estate and business development, management of Fountain Square by 3CDC included promotion of the square as a "premier destination location." Promotion of seasonal activities (ice skating, broomball games) and holiday events (July 4th fireworks, Octoberfest), music and dancing specialty events ("Salsa on the Square," "Acoustic Thursday," "Reggae Wednesday"), and the erection of a jumbo LED video screen reportedly brought thousands of visitors downtown yearround (Cincinnati Center City Development Corporation, 2010b, p. 2). 3CDC vigorously promoted the square, using expertise from entertainment, concert production, and theme park management.

The extension of authority for 3CDC to issue use permits did not come to public attention until the spring of 2007, when the Intercommunity Justice and Peace Center, led by Sister Alice Gerdeman, requested a permit for an antiwar demonstration on Fountain Square. The group's plans were thwarted by newly established policies and prohibitive fees. The new fees included extraordinarily high-priced purchased insurance indemnity, which had previously been lower and covered in part by the city but was now not covered by 3CDC. The demonstration was not held, and the request was soon followed by denial by 3CDC of a request from the Homeless Youth Empowerment Council of Greater Cincinnati to use Fountain Square for a Saturday afternoon summer job fair. The youths were initially denied a permit as their chosen date conflicted with a permit taken for a flower show: the "Great Pansy Display." All alternative dates requested by the youths were also taken by the flower show, for 29 days in April. These two groups soon discovered that there was no real appeal process for contesting or negotiating these decisions made by the authority of 3CDC.

These Fountain Square permit denials and obstacles might have gone unnoticed but for the great Bearcat dust-up of October 6, 2007. The University of Cincinnati Bearcat football team was playing Rutgers in a sold-out game during their then all-time "winningest" season. At the same time, perennial winners the Ohio State Buckeyes were playing Purdue. Sure enough, the collegiate game that 3CDC decided to show on the Fountain Square jumbo LED screen affixed to the east side of Macy's facing the square was the Ohio State game. The decision to show the Ohio State game was made by 3CDC's Fountain Square managing director Bill Donabedian. Bearcat fans were outraged and let their displeasure be known: Irate e-mails called for Donabedian's head; others accused him of being clueless about the city (as if he were not a Cincinnatian). The *Enquirer* front-page headline screamed "Fountain Square snub riles up Bearcat fans" (Dow, 2007). Donabedian apologized, admitting he had decided to show the Ohio State game as a matter of personal privilege for a friend. He added that in the future, 3CDC "will accommodate requests if the big screen isn't being used for a specific purpose." It took this dust-up over a college football game to reveal how decisions concerning public access to public space were now to be made—use of nonnegotiable, prohibitive fees for public antiwar speech; "blacked-out" dates accommodating flats of pansies over a youth afternoon job fair; and, perhaps most insulting to the public, personal privilege for a friend.

These thwarted attempts for use of Fountain Square probably brought harm to no one and were not pursued as First Amendment rights, as in the religious symbol cases previously fought. They could be dismissed for bringing no benefit to economic development—a peaceful antiwar demonstration led by a nun, homeless kids with punk outfits and tattooed forearms looking for summer jobs, a bunch of beer-drinking Bearcat football fans. However, the thwarting of permits does raise very serious questions about who is privileged to make decisions on use of public space and, of equal importance, what protections are in place for grievance or appeal of decisions made by the private assets manager. To be clear, the privatized contract to manage the square is not a contract to provide some quantity of certain goods or measureable services sought by the city. Unlike the purchase of supplies or services ranging from office supplies to fire trucks or street paving, the purchase of planning, economic development, and asset management does not lie in needs as identified by the city. Nor does it lie in contracting for development and management of the city's plan for valued public assets, and it certainly does not lie in the community's public access needs. Instead, planning authority and decisions are yielded to a private contractor, with the intended effect being the advancement of the contractor's plan, not the city's plan.

Exaggerated Crime Crisis and Privatization of Planning and Economic Development

The second arena of influence of 3CDC was the privatization of authority for planning and economic development in OTR initiated with the establishment of 3CDC in July 2003. At the time, the socioeconomic–political climate surrounding OTR reflected decades of contentious relationships; persistent media portrayal of OTR as a crime-ridden, drug-infested community; and contentious power struggles wildly fluctuating between developers (strongly influenced by the arts community) and community activists (historically portrayed as "poverty pimps," supposedly working to keep OTR poor). The emotional context for this picture of OTR paralleled the recent national history of social and cultural changes related to an anticrime, welfare reform, conservative social agenda. Passions were inflamed by the portrayal of OTR as the most dangerous of the city's 52 neighborhoods in 2003 when police calls for service (22,993) (Cincinnati Police Department, 2004) exceeded population (9,572) (City of Cincinnati Planning Commission, 2002b), as if that ratio was meaningful. Many of these calls for service were related to drug dealing and prostitution in open-air markets on street corners. Few of the customers or dealers were residents of OTR but, rather, were from other communities of the tri-state area.

Heightened police patrols had produced increased arrests, fueling the perception of rising crime. In the spring of 2001, police shot and killed Timothy Thomas, a 19-year-old African American, as he fled on foot across backyard fences on Republic Street in OTR. He was wanted on outstanding traffic warrants and was the 15th African American man killed at the hands of the police in seven years. What were subsequently termed "riots" ensued, causing some property damage—a few broken storefront windows, torched garbage cans and dumpsters, and street demonstrations by those described as "gangs of youths." Many in the community, especially those who had witnessed local civil unrest during the 1960s at the height of the Civil Rights movement, questioned whether these were much more than episodes of youthful vandalism or a minor civil disturbance. The mayor called a citywide curfew over the April 2001 Easter holiday weekend, soon restoring order but drawing national media attention, with repetitive cable television reports intensifying the reputation of OTR as among the most dangerous of American urban areas.

Prior to the shooting of Timothy Thomas, a class action suit had been filed by the American Civil Liberties Union in federal court against the city of Cincinnati, the Police Department, and the Fraternal Order of Police on behalf of "all African-American or Black persons and people who reside, work in and/or travel on public thoroughfares in Cincinnati . . . who have been subjected to use of force by Cincinnati police officers and their agents." This precedent-setting case was settled by an extraordinary court-supervised collaborative agreement (*In re: Cincinnati Policing*, 2001) made between the citizens, the city, and the Fraternal Order of Police to reform police practices, to engage all parties in community problem-oriented policing, and to evaluate improvements in community–police relationships, police training and protocols, and engagement of the community. This remarkable civic milestone in city policing and citizen participation has thoroughly evaluated and documented, and reviewing it is beyond the scope of this work. However, it is important to understand the impact of this case on the heightened social and political sensitivities in OTR at the time.

More than a year after the collaborative agreement was signed and significant improvements in community–police relations were resulting from its implementation, national press coverage continued to report high crime in American cities, singling out Cincinnati with headlines such as *USA Today*'s "Crime Keeps Cincinnati Reeling" (Johnson, 2002) and citing double-digit increases in crimes of homicide, rape, and crack and cocaine offenses.

Coincident with the heightened fervor regarding crime in OTR was impassioned, policy-driven decision making pertaining to housing and economic development, the former driven by debate over how to use federal funds (CDBG, HOME) for affordable housing in a classic conflict between development of affordable or upscale housing, the latter driven by momentum to relocate and build a new public high school for the performing arts and save Music Hall, the city-owned home of the renowned Cincinnati Symphony Orchestra, the May Festival, and the Cincinnati Opera.

The momentum to build a new building in OTR for the public high school, the SCPA, included a drive to remove social services from their established locations near sites proposed for the school. As described in chapter 8, the prime targets for removal were the DIC, transitional housing programs, and soup kitchens in proximity of Music Hall and Washington Park.

The OTR community was still stung by the loss of ReStoc's Vine Street Community Project, followed by the setback to affordable housing development and rehabilitation brought on by the Housing Impaction Ordinance (both described in detail in chapters 7 and 8). In addition, changes in HUD's funding policies for assisted housing, which had been shifted from project-based assistance to landlords with HUD mortgages to vouchers issued to tenants, were affecting both landlords and tenants. Undergirding these planning and economic development issues and conflicts, and intensifying the process of econocide, was the shelving of the *Over-the-Rhine Comprehensive Plan,* only six months after it had been adopted in June 2002. Loss of the plan, in concert with the elimination of the Planning Department, left the community with no provision for recourse on planning and development decisions. The market-driven reversal of the ReStoc's Vine Street housing plan had heralded the subsequent market-driven takeover of other affordable housing, such a Race Street SRO building and the Metropole Apartments, for development by 3CDC. Authority for such decisions had been shifted to 3CDC.

This socioeconomic–political climate in OTR at the time of 3CDC's initiation in mid-2003 could be described as a battleground for a relentless, policy-driven removal of economic others by relentlessly indentifying them as criminal and deviant, reducing or eliminating the social services some depended on for survival, eliminating their place in the emerging market economy, and denying their options to seek redress with their government. These actions were supplemented by powerful efforts to develop OTR with upscale housing, new businesses, and private management of public assets.

Each policy initiative that was part of this process, from the panhandling and drug-exclusion ordinances to the efforts at development of the inner city, viewed in isolation, could be seen as having merit in its time and within a specific context—to reduce drug trafficking by removing drug offenders, to promote housing choices by shifting housing assistance from projects to tenants, to promote arts education by constructing a new arts school, and so on. However, when considered together, they formed a relentless, often unacknowledged attack on the presence of economic others in and around the OTR community. Often overtly directed at certain people or groups (privileged or poor) in the community, such initiatives were manifest in public policy decisions and use of resources of the city that ruthlessly exploited socioeconomic dichotomies—affordable housing or upscale housing, arts schools or shelters for the homeless, federal assistance for affordable housing or public investment for upscale housing, arbitrary zoning changes or community-based planning—with little attention to possibility that coexistence of social and economic interests could be effected. The net effect, over time, was a relentless, econocidal removal of those least able to participate in market economies by those who have the greatest influence on market economies.

Property Acquisition, Land-Banking, and De Facto Eminent Domain

The ability to initiate regulatory reform, issue bonds, and use eminent domain given to 3CDC by the city gave the public–private partnership the power needed to be the exclusive planner and developer for OTR. In a more equitable scenario, planning for OTR could have been based on the *Over-the-Rhine Comprehensive Plan*, now "shelved" with the dissolution of the Planning Department. Although 3CDC acknowledged the *Plan* in its first-year report, claiming to have "established . . . OTR as a vibrant, mixed income, diverse urban neighborhood in accordance with the OTR Comprehensive Plan" (Cincinnati Center City Development Corporation, 2004, p. 3), none of 3CDC's other accomplishments cited in that first year were elements of the *Plan*. 3CDC's plans were clearly different from what the larger community had agreed to with the *Over-the-Rhine Comprehensive Plan*. The CDC recommended in the *Over-the-Rhine Comprehensive Plan* had been supplanted by the business-driven public–private partnership that became 3CDC, not an "umbrella Community Development Corporation" with broad representation from resident as well as development interests (City of Cincinnati Planning Commission, 2002b).

Further, planning for and development of an established, built-out community raised important issues of development of mostly private property on privately held land. For more than a century, OTR has had virtually no vacant land. Significant public spaces in OTR include Music Hall, owned by the city; Memorial Hall (veterans memorial), owned by the county; Findlay Market, a public market owned by the city; Washington Park, Zeigler pool, Hanna pool, and the Over-the-Rhine Recreation Center, owned by the city; and three public schools, Rothenberg (grades K–8), the former Washington Park Elementary (now removed, with the land added to Washington Park), and the SCPA (grades K–12 in the new building). The balance of land use is privately held housing (mostly multiunit buildings); retail storefront space with housing above; vacant land parcels; and industrial space previously housing breweries, small factories, and commercial concerns.

In 2002, the *Over-the-Rhine Comprehensive Plan* projected a potential capacity of 7,500 housing units, beginning with the 5,261 habitable units found by the 2000 U.S. Census, adding 1,250 by renovation, 300 new units, and nearly 500 by conversion. At the same time, the plan verified 1,667 vacant housing units and 703 vacant land parcels, mostly small, 2,000 to 3,000 square feet (City of Cincinnati Planning Commission, 2002b). The OTR population in the 2000 Census was 7,422 (down from 9,572 in 1990 and 11,914 in 1980), with a median household income of $9,024 (the city's median household income for the same year was nearly three-and-a-half times as much: $32,278). When OTR was handed over to 3CDC for development in 2003, it was an old neighborhood with aging, privately held housing stock and a plummeting population of people who were poor, many of whom were economic others living in a neighborhood with a wealth of public assets and a paucity of vacant land. Most of the vacant spaces were small building lots (a standard city lot measuring 25 feet by 125 feet is 3,125 square feet, making such space among the largest of the 703 vacant lots in OTR). The housing stock, considered one of the nation's largest stocks of Italianate style architecture with historic designation, was, in many ways, a developer's dream—coveted buildings at rock-bottom prices in an historic, artsy district ripe for "buy low, sell high" conversion to urban upscale, condominium-trendy apartments within walking distance to retail and entertainment venues and the downtown corporate offices of Fortune 500 companies.

Six years later, in 2009, 3CDC had acquired a substantial portfolio of properties in OTR, held by its subsidiary, OTR Holdings, Inc. Most of the properties held by 3CDC are vacant and boarded-up apartment buildings land-banked for future development. Previously, when the neighborhood's nonprofit housing development corporation ReStoc used a similar strategy to purchase vacant property to hold until sufficient funds and volunteer labor could be raised for rehabilitation, it was accused of stockpiling to keep the neighborhood poor.

Land-banking to hold properties for development of upscale housing is apparently not regarded with the same scorn.

The 3CDC holdings include some properties purchased from private landlords, such as the 2006 purchase of 1316–1318 Race Street that was home to 16 to 18 economically poor tenants renting SRO units. The terms of the sale required the seller to vacate the building prior to closing, displacing 20 people, who immediately joined the ranks of economic others. Five were known to have turned to shelters (Cincinnati/Hamilton County Continuum of Care, Inc., 2010a); the others turned to the street or the riverbank or transiency. The largest 3CDC acquisition was the purchase of the Tom Denhart properties after his bankruptcy, vacant units soon to be boarded up and land-banked. At this writing, OTR Holdings, Inc., inventory, per the Hamilton County auditor's records (see http://hamiltoncountyauditor.org/), includes 162 properties in OTR. As there are few single-family houses in OTR, these holdings represent a substantial number of units for redevelopment in buildings of 8 to 40 units, potentially fewer if used for conversation to condominium-style housing. Although holding this huge inventory of buildings in OTR, 3CDC also acted with the city of Cincinnati and HUD for a planned acquisition of the Metropole Apartments in the nearby downtown area, purchased when the former owner opted out of a decades-old HUD mortgage.

Whether acquired by purchase by a private holding company with public money, for purposes of land-banking as in OTR, or for purposes of private economic development using public money as with the Metropole Apartments, such policy-supported transactions are tantamount to taking private property by public acts for private purposes, driven by the market, not the public good. Because 3CDC is a private corporation, and the properties were purchased by private financial transactions, although publicly funded, the city's powers of eminent domain were not needed in these acts of de facto eminent domain. These actions bring to mind the words of Lemkin (1944) defining the elements of genocide: "a coordinated plan of different actions aiming at the destruction of essential foundation of the life of [national] groups, with the aim of annihilating the groups themselves" (p. 79).

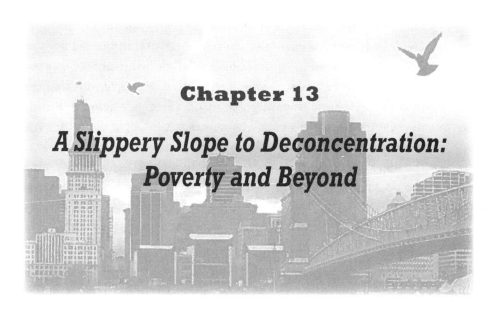

Chapter 13

A Slippery Slope to Deconcentration: Poverty and Beyond

As previously described, the concept of deconcentrating poverty was introduced into the narrative on housing policy in Cincinnati with the passage of the Housing Impaction Ordinance (Cincinnati City Council, 2001) in late 2001. Although the explicit intent of the ordinance was worded in phrases like "reduce the concentration of poverty," "rehabilitate vacant and abandoned buildings," and "oppose the construction of new publicly-assisted low-income rental unless construction reduces the concentration of poverty," the implicit intent was to remove and not replace the places where people who were poor, especially economic others, lived in neighborhoods supposedly affected by poverty. As the following examples illustrate, policies to "reduce concentrations of poverty" and promote economic homogeneity were inevitable. The envisioned economic homogeneity could not accommodate economic poverty.

With passage and implementation of the Housing Impaction Ordinance, public discourse began to reflect fait accompli notions surrounding the social and moral acceptability and irreversibility of abolishing certain kinds of housing (especially rent-assisted housing) to facilitate the removal of certain kinds of people (those who are poor, those who are homeless, and economic others). Implementation of the ordinance was immediate, beginning with allocation decisions in the next round of HUD funding in the CDBG, HOME, and Emergency Shelter Grant (ESG) programs, with changes made immediately to the City's *Consolidated Plan* only because of HUD requirements.

In gradual and sometimes subtle shifts, housing policy notions of deconcentrating poverty by removal of affordable housing began to shift beyond housing to the deconcentration of social services used by those who are poor. It was but a small step to the notion that removing services used by people who are poor would advance their removal from neighborhoods where they, along with their services, were concentrated. This notion became especially applicable to removal of economic others who were served by private, voluntary services, street-level services like soup kitchens, shelters, and food pantries. The DIC shelter became a target for deconcentration of social services under the guise of safety for students of the yet-to-be-built SCPA, which was seen as being threatened by day use of the adjacent Washington Park by economic others. Public, categorical services like welfare, Social Security, housing assistance, and health clinics were cited with less frequency.

Ideas of deconcentrating social services began to appear in City Council proceedings and city documents such as the letter to the City Council entered as public record by prominent attorney John W. Hauck (2004). Hauck wrote to the City Council regarding the plan for renovation of Fountain Square, citing it as misguided if its purpose was to enhance retail business, as he claimed Fountain Square was not a destination point for visitors. By comparison, facetiously referencing the Washington Park area, he continued:

> A poor comparison is Washington Park. All jokes aside, the poor and homeless flood Washington Park on a daily basis, especially along 12th Street, for a specific reason. They come there from the *adjoining* social service agencies. There is nothing special about Washington Park that attracts them simply due to the beauty of the park. They are there for other reasons. Take away the social service agencies, and Washington Park would have far fewer visitors on a daily basis. (Hauck, 2004, p. 4)

Although Hauck's comparison of Fountain Square visitation with daily usage of Washington Park was obscure, it did herald policy ideas about alleged usage of the park by those who use nearby social services.

Discussions about the park were inflamed by demands for relocation of two properties owned by DIC then being used for transitional housing programs on land needed for construction of the new school. The demand for the land made by the private group raising funds for SCPA included, by association, a blatant call for removal of park users reputed to be homeless, panhandling, derelict DIC clients for the safety of school children in the yet-to-be-built school building.

As the demands for DIC-owned land escalated, city funding for DIC for the year 2008 was withheld pending certain "improvements" demanded by the City Council. Those demands were eventually resolved; however, language in the DIC funding allocation agreement included the following:

> In this program DIC implemented an intensive case management program designed to serve homeless individuals . . . a marked decrease in the chronically homeless and bed nights used in emergency shelter. . . . The new service program scheduled to begin in February 2008 and *it is expected to continue to facilitate the goal of de-concentration of homelessness from the Washington Park area* [italics added]. (Dohoney, 2008, pp. 8–9)

Emphasis is added to highlight the goal of "deconcentration of homelessness." Like deconcentration of poverty and deconcentration of social services, with this contract the narrative had expanded to include deconcentration of homelessness.

Ideas of deconcentration of social services surfaced in 2006 when a group of church-related volunteers operating under the name CityLink proposed a bold new social service facility. Widely advertized in a glossy marketing brochure as a multipurpose social service center, it was to be located in the West End neighborhood, adjacent to OTR. CityLink purchased an empty warehouse and proposed to use it for shelter for the homeless, transitional housing, job training, ex-offender services, health services, and emergency assistance, in an ambitious plan advertised as a "social services mall," at a cost of $15 million. Margaret Wuerstle (2009), chief planner for the city, described this project as "the 'tipping point' that forced the City to pursue stricter regulations for social service facilities . . . addressing the overarching issues associated with regulation of social service agencies through municipal ordinances and zoning regulations" (p. 33).

CityLink's proposed usage and zoning for the development of the warehouse was initially approved by the city as conforming to the City Code in a location zoned for "manufacturing, general." The proposed usage was immediately opposed by the West End neighborhood, including the Community Council, residents, local churches, and social agencies and, curiously, by developers from OTR, including the OTR Foundation and the Chamber of Commerce, even though the site was not in OTR. West End neighborhood opposition was clearly expressed by West End resident Christopher McCarty (2005), as he wrote to the City Council citing the proposed mall's proximity to three schools, saying that that the "center will no doubt become a magnet for the homeless, drug users, and inmates freshly released out of prison."

Similarly, Marge Hammelrath (2006), then executive director of the OTR Foundation, subsidiary of the OTR Chamber of Commerce, wrote to the City Council, sweeping OTR and the West End broadly into the "inner city," fearing for the downtown and the entire city and requesting that the city stop the West End CityLink project:

> The inner city, whether it be Over-the-Rhine or the West End are inundated with social services, and we feel that any other, however well meaning will only continue the draw to the downtown area people with extreme needs. . . . The location is just one of the concerns that needs to be dealt with, but the size is of utmost concern as well. If we are to attract even more people to Ohio, and Cincinnati in particular, this means that however successful CityLink is in helping people to avoid their demons, they will most likely remain within the City of Cincinnati. This is something we need to address if our City is to continue to succeed in attracting tax-paying residents and businesses.

Both McCarty's and Hammelrath's communications were entered into City Council's records and deliberations on this zoning issue. Approval of CityLink's proposal was granted.

Opponents, led by the West End Community Council, appealed to the Zoning Board of Appeals, who overturned the city's approval. CityLink then carried the decision to the Common Pleas Court and the Hamilton County Court of Appeals, where the city's initial approval permitting the social services mall was upheld and zoned with a "manufacturing, general" code. CityLink had argued that, as each of the proposed uses (shelter, transitional housing, job training, and so on) was a permitted use in "manufacturing, general" zoning, so the combination of human services (the mall) uses in one site should be permitted. Initially the city approved that interpretation, then rescinded it, only to lose on appeal. However, this case called into question the use of the existing codes and raised the larger issue of using zoning codes for the regulation of social services.

Opponents of CityLink, including the OTR developers, had succeeded in reframing discussion of the CityLink project, portraying it as "community service facility" that, if allowed, would open the way for the city to approve social services in any zone; services such as soup kitchens, shelters for the homeless, and recovery programs could be approved anywhere, even in affluent areas and residential zones. The CityLink project proceeded, but not without consequences for the future of social service zoning.

This episode—inflamed by rhetoric demeaning poor neighborhoods, economic others, *and* social services—succeeded in shifting the policy narrative from the deconcentration of poverty to deconcentration of social services. The City Council responded to the appeals court decision by passing a resolution titled "Revised Resolution–CityLink," directing the city administration to "adhere to the policy that social services agencies and programming shall not be concentrated in a single geographic area and shall not locate in an area deemed impacted" (Cincinnati City Council, 2008b). The rhetoric of the resolution singled out OTR as having an "unchecked proliferation of agencies":

> WHEREAS, there is an unusually large number of social service agencies in the Over the Rhine area of the City of Cincinnati;
>
> WHEREAS, the unchecked proliferation of these agencies has the potential to negatively impact the residential character and the neighborhood serving commercial uses of Over the Rhine;

This shifted the deconcentration narrative beyond the ordinary "not in my backyard" response often raised when assisted housing or social services are proposed for residential neighborhoods, for it now expanded the supposed negative impact of such services to include "neighborhood-serving" commercial uses. The narrative stew of competing interests now included neighborhood, development interests, faith traditions, housing, social services, and commerce.

The resolution continued with several clauses referencing the CityLink zoning code approval in the "manufacturing, general" zone, with an astonishing statement paraphrasing sections of the *Municipal Code* (City of Cincinnati, 2010):

> WHEREAS, under the Zoning Code, permitted uses in Manufacturing subdistricts do not include either "Community Service Facilities," which include offices of non-profit civil, religious, welfare, or philanthropic organizations, or "Special Assistance Shelters," which are defined as "facilities for the short term housing for individuals who are homeless and who may require special services," or "Religious Assembly," which includes religious education, rectories and parsonages, offices, social services, columbaria and community programs:

And yet another:

> WHEREAS, City Council's current policy is to reduce the concentration of poverty through homeownership and oppose the construction of

transitional or rental housing unless it reduces the concentration of poverty or is intended for occupancy by the elderly;

The body of the resolution declared it the policy of the city of Cincinnati that "social service agencies and programming shall not be concentrated in a single geographic area and not in an area deemed impacted which at this time includes Over the Rhine" and instructed the city Manager to implement such a policy and "use his authority, to the extent permitted by law, to carryout actions required" (City of Cincinnati Department of City Planning, 2008a).

City administration recognized that if the city manager were to implement deconcentration of social services as required by the ordinance, codes pertaining to social services would be needed in the *Municipal Code*. The administration responded by convening a Social Services Committee (SSC) with membership representative of the community, social service providers, businesses, and CityLink. Convened under the auspices of the City Planning Department and staffed by the chief planner, the SSC was charged with making recommendations to the Planning Commission in four areas: (1) identification of existing providers and their best practices; (2) impact of social service uses and concentration in neighborhoods; (3) zoning and writing definitions of social services; and (4) church–religious land use, with attention paid to the federal Religious Land Use and Institutionalized Persons Act of 2000 (RLUIPA).

The work plan set for the committee contained 23 items, ranging from definitions of community service facility, social services, transitional housing, special assistance shelter, to districts where social services should be permitted, to adherence to RLUIPA and enforcement of limitations on social services (City of Cincinnati Department of City Planning, 2008b). The committee met in 19 contentious meetings. Members were clearly divided into opposing factions: those who openly sought removal of all social services from OTR and those who wanted to preserve or refine the existing City Zoning Code so that providers of social services could continue to meet the needs of economic others with community-based services. Some wanted to remove approval for the faith-based CityLink programs, and others wanted to remove social services from OTR that had originated with faith-based groups previously known as churches, synagogues, and mosques, not social service malls. These opposing, firmly held positions raised the RLUIPA discussion to particularly contentious levels. Planning staff provided written clarification regarding RLUIPA from the city solicitor as it pertained to the city:

> As long as zoning regulations are used to regulate completely secular ancillary uses of property by churches, those regulations may not be deemed

violations of RLUIPA. However, as ancillary uses become tied in with religion, e.g., a church-run homeless shelter that offers faith-based counseling, their regulation becomes more suspect under RLUIPA. (McNeil, 2006)

The committee's work, as presented to the Planning Commission for approval and transmittal to the City Council to amend the City Zoning Code, included 29 text amendments. The amendments included 11 revisions to definitions, one new definition (soup kitchen—full service), and 15 use regulation revisions pertaining to social services. Two zoning text amendments are of particular note. Section 1401-01-H7 proposed a new definition titled "Human Service Multi-use Centers," for services like CityLink, with the following justification:

> To address the large center that provides integrated services to their clients
> . . . that one-stop centers should be regulated differently than transitional/
> supportive housing uses and human service facilities as these centers may
> provide services to on-site residential clients as well as other individual that
> are not using the on-site services. (City of Cincinnati Department of City
> Planning, 2008b)

The other significant amendment concerned a proposed definition of religious assembly, removing all references to religious education, rectories, parsonages, social services, columbaria, and so on. Section 1401-01-R7, "Religious Assembly," was retained as "Religious Assembly means an establishment for religious worship and other religious ceremonies."

With the completion of the work of the SSC and the zoning text amendments regulating social services forwarded to, but not yet adopted by, the Planning Commission, nor sent to City Council for approval, Resolution No. 41-2008 was challenged in federal court by a group of social service advocates, agencies, and the Greater Cincinnati Coalition for the Homeless. (Full disclosure: I am one of the plaintiffs). The complaint challenged the resolution's legality on grounds of violation of due process, equal protection, First Amendment protections, and land use in OTR. The city filed a motion to dismiss, claiming that the resolution is not an ordinance and, therefore, does not have the force and effect of a law. Plaintiffs' lawyer, Tim Burke, filed a motion in opposition to the motion to dismiss, pointing out that "the intended impact of the Resolution is to reduce the availability of social services in an area of the City where they are most needed— Over-the-Rhine" (T. M. Burke, personal communication, November 29, 2008).

The plaintiffs argued that the resolution had been adopted in retaliation against agencies that spoke against the proposed "new restrictive zoning regulations that had not been evaluated by the Planning Commission" and, if implemented, "would limit the delivery of services, particularly in Over-the-Rhine" (T. M. Burke, personal communication, April 16, 2010). District judge Herman J. Weber ruled in favor of the city to dismiss the complaint, a ruling later upheld by the magistrate, judge Timothy S. Black (*Greater Cincinnati Coalition for the Homeless et al. v. City of Cincinnati*, 2008, 2010). The court upheld the resolution that it is the policy of the city of Cincinnati that "social services shall not be concentrated in a single geographic area and not in an area deemed impacted, which at this time includes Over-the-Rhine."

The relentless policy-driven march to remove economic others from areas like OTR persists by use of the resolution to effect deconcentration of social services. As of mid-2011, the zoning text amendments had not been fully approved by the Planning Commission or forwarded to the City Council for adoption. The definition of religious assembly remains unchanged, the CityLink project proceeds, and efforts to remove the DIC and those who use Washington Park continue in the name of deconcentration of poverty, housing, social services, removing those who are poor and economic others for the sake of economic homogeneity.

Chapter 14

Considerable Community Debate . . . about Homeless Shelters

During the decade-long battle between community and development interests, with the DIC as a repeated flashpoint, 3CDC had often been praised in the media, with comments such as "3CDC's strategy of buying properties that have been breeding grounds for crime has already paid dividends" (Bernard-Kuhn, 2009c, p. 6). Such praise extended over several years, with one headline proclaiming "Plan to Fix Washington Park Good for Children, Neighbors" (2007). At the same time, from a viewpoint across several social divides of class and race in OTR, 3CDC has also been described in the media as

> urban messiahs sent from the powers of corporate heaven, to save the masses from the plagues and pestilence of homelessness, poverty, and other unsightly unmentionables that exist in Over-the-Rhine. 3CDC and the other market-rate developers have been sent to OTR to bring the rich white folks in and to ship out the poor black ones. With high-cost condos, fancy French bistros and upscale furniture stores, the residents of OTR are being made strangers in their own neighborhood. It is a shame that 3CDC's vision for Over-the-Rhine does not include the people who already live here. (D'Intino, 2007, p. D2)

Despite these markedly antithetical views, inflamed by public narrative crossing gaping social divides, the city's policy actions pointed to a one-dimensional solution: the DIC brings homelessness to the park that impedes market development and threatens safety of school children, which necessitates the removal of "home-lessness" from the park and, therefore, requires immediate removal of the DIC.

As discussed earlier, notions of deconcentration of poverty had propelled poli-cies that prevented use of public funds for affordable housing and had expanded to attempts to deconcentrate social services in poor neighborhoods, especially OTR, by altering zoning codes. In simultaneous efforts, these notions were extended beyond the geographical boundaries of OTR. Codified as deconcen-tration of homelessness and to further decrease the incidence of homelessness within the city, they were written into contracts for ESGs for all shelters and pro-grams serving homeless individuals and families. Thus, it became city policy to require that all shelters receiving federal ESG funding were to decrease homeless-ness in the city. Although decreasing the incidence of homelessness could be seen as a legitimate goal for the city, writing it into contracts for services for homeless populations seemed a major non sequitur—decreasing homelessness seems a function of increasing homes and housing, not regulation of temporary shelters. Shelters were being asked to reduce the very populations they were contracting to serve—the likely intent no doubt was removal of homeless people.

By late 2008, policy extensions of deconcentration deepened and congealed in Emergency Ordinance 347-2008, which came to be known as the Homeless to Homes Ordinance. This ordinance later resulted in the *Homeless to Homes* report (Cincinnati/Hamilton County Continuum of Care, Inc., 2009) and *The Homeless to Homes Plan* (Cincinnati/Hamilton County Continuum of Care, Inc., 2010b), adopted by the City Council in subsequent ordinances.

The Homeless to Homes Ordinance directed the CoC, the public–private partnership operated as a nonprofit corporation charged with planning and implementation of services for the homeless, to "immediately address the inad-equacies of the current provision of services for single homeless individuals in the City of Cincinnati." The CoC, by its own description, is an artifact of HUD policies "designed to help communities develop the capacity to plan and imple-ment long-term solutions to homelessness for their jurisdictions" (Cincinnati City Council, 2008a). Organized and incorporated in 2007 and functioning as a quasi-governmental agency, CoC, as described in the Homeless to Homes Ordinance, "operates a *single, coordinated and inclusive process* for planning and management of the local homeless housing and services, as required by the U.S. Department of Housing and Urban Development." The CoC's "coordinated and inclusive process" is embodied in the Homeless Clearinghouse, a decision-making body with voting representation from the city and county Departments of Com-munity Development, the Greater Cincinnati Coalition for the Homeless, and

elected representatives from the CoC working groups (providers of specific services such as family shelters, street outreach, permanent supportive housing, and
transitional housing). The Homeless Clearinghouse used a HUD-approved
model that originated with a less formal local process, in which providers priori-
tized funding and services using peer-based consensus, called the "Prince of Peace
Process," so named because its organizational meetings in the mid-1980s took
place in the undercroft of the Prince of Peace Lutheran Church in OTR. Having
been organized by providers with representation from public and private providers of services and funders, the process built a consensus foundation for planning
and funding decisions carried forward to the CoC.

The CoC is now charged with planning and coordinating services and programs for those who are homeless, upholding the City's *Consolidated Plan*, and
supporting use of resources to "improve the quality of life for homeless persons
and/or to end homelessness." Organizationally, it is similar to 3CDC but without
regulatory or bonding authority. The Homeless to Homes Ordinance required
the CoC to prepare a comprehensive plan that guarantees the "highest standards
of service for the homeless," ensuring that all recommendations of the plan "must
insure that any facilities are 'Good Neighbors' and do not result in any behavior
or actions that are disruptive to businesses and residents."

The ordinance establishes the expertise of CoC, citing its outstanding performance according to HUD evaluations, including preparation of the city's
Consolidated Plan, and the ability of the city to draw on federal funds because
both CoC performance and the *Consolidated Plan* "exceed national expectations."
Conditions of homelessness were reported, including the number of homeless
people in the city in 2007 (7,298) and the number of emergency shelter beds for
single individuals (312) in four identified shelters. The ordinance referenced a
separate county request to privatize the Mt. Airy Center (a city-owned, county-
operated, 70-year-old municipal shelter housing up to 65 homeless single men
per night, many with substance abuse problems, in obsolete Civilian Conservation Corps camp buildings in the city's Mt. Airy Forest), removing it from the
county's budget *and* responsibilities. The clause references community debate
about DIC:

> WHEREAS, the Hamilton County Department of Job and Family Ser-
> vices believes that the direct provision of shelter at Mt. Airy Center is not
> within their core competencies and have requested a process be developed
> to privatize Mt. Airy Center and *in consideration of the considerable commu-
> nity debate about the Drop Inn Center* [italics added], now therefore . . .

The ordinance stipulates that a *Homeless to Homes Plan* be completed within 90 days, making recommendations to ensure that single men and women have access to safe, appropriate shelters; that all facilities are "good neighbors" (do not result in any behavior or actions that are disruptive to businesses and residents); that shelter services are modeled on "best practices"; that providers and funding are determined by objective, competitive processes; and that the CoC include specified stakeholders in the planning process.

CoC organized a Homeless to Homes Steering Committee and began to research the needs of single homeless individuals. Homeless families and their services were not included in this effort—in fact, they were specifically written out of the ordinance so that the focus could be exclusively on shelters for single homeless men and women. For some, the puzzling omission of shelters for homeless families to focus solely on such a few shelters and programs for homeless single people made it but a short step to conclude that the ordinance was written to facilitate the removal of DIC from its location in OTR and "deconcentrate" homeless singles to other locations and programs. Shifting the old municipal Mt. Airy Shelter from the county budget to federal funding through a purchase of service contract with a private provider seemed a secondary concern. The ordinance also added credence to a rumored relocation of the 50 beds of the faith-based City Gospel Mission (not counted in the city's portfolio because it receives no federal funds) from its OTR location, then on prime property within 3CDC's sphere of redevelopment. The Mission was established in 1924 in OTR, moving to its Elm Street location in 1943, two blocks north of DIC, now being removed from OTR in the name of the Homeless to Homes plan, providing a convenient "rationale" to advance 3CDC's plans.

The CoC approved the Steering Committee's list of research topics for subcommittees to address: homeless young adults, single women, single men, street outreach, permanent supportive and transitional housing, mental health and substance abuse best practices, and funding. (Full disclosure: I chaired the Women's Committee for the study.) The work of the subcommittees was statistics laden and policy driven, grounded in underlying assumptions of the policy worthiness of privatization. It drew on years of data accumulated through the CoC-operated, federally mandated HMIS and city and county statistics on jails and incarcerations and arrests surrounding shelters, and it was grounded in underlying assumptions of the policy worthiness of privatization. Existing related privatization efforts (privatize the municipal shelter), upscale economic development of OTR, and locating and building the new SCPA provided a template for developing the recommendations that were to follow. CoC delivered the *Homeless to*

Homes Report to the City Council in the required 90 days; City Council adopted the report and appointed an implementation team, both by ordinance (Cincinnati City Council, 2009).

A detailed account of the recommendations of the *Homeless to Homes Report* is beyond the scope of this work and would add little to the import of its implementation. Major portions of the report documented the critical need for transitional and permanent supportive housing for homeless populations, especially for those with addictions or diagnoses of mental illness. Implementation of the recommendations from the report that directly affect OTR, and the shelters for singles located in OTR, entailed significant changes in operations, direct services, and locations of shelters, rather than heeding the clear priority for development of housing.

Implicit in the report are recommendations that point to a takeover of shelter services, rather than recommendations that "immediately address the inadequacies of the current provision of services for single homeless individuals in the City of Cincinnati," as it was purported to be. Like a business takeover that acquires a controlling interest in a firm, often despite resistance of the firm's board or management, the recommendations adopted by the City Council in *The Homeless to Homes Report* set in motion not only decisions about management and location of shelters and postshelter housing for homeless singles, but also standards for operations and best practice models required for public funding. In effect, planning services, allocation of public funds, and even prescription of what professional social service models will be used for homeless services had been transferred to CoC, a public–private partnership driven by obdurate policies of the City Council for promotion of economic homogeneity.

The Homeless to Homes plan is now incorporated in the city and county 2010–2014 *Consolidated Plan*. Implementation proceeds, with three priority actions pertaining to shelter operations and location (Cincinnati/Hamilton County Continuum of Care, Inc., 2009):

+ Establish a transition team for implementation of the recommendations transitioned "so as not to cause additional hardships for homeless individuals or result in an increase in street homelessness."
+ Undertake additional efforts to identify Best Practices and medical services for the homeless . . . [establish] service delivery models and programs that achieve notable success.
+ Recognize community concern over safety related to the location of shelter. Minimum Standards for Shelter must be developed and shelters must

then pledge to adhere to those standards for public funding . . . new shelters should not be sited next door to, across the street from, or adjacent to an existing school. Definition of "school" and "adjacent to" must be clearly defined and researched. Further, the transitional process must address the safety factors in locating new shelters in the future. (pp. 1–2)

Specific recommendations from the *Report* (Cincinnati/Hamilton County Continuum of Care, Inc., 2009, pp. 5–6) include reconfiguration of men's shelters to be no more than 50 beds in small sleeping rooms, not open, dormitory-style large rooms; separation of women's shelters from men's shelters; expansion of the current inventory of transitional and permanent supportive housing options not to include any in Census Tract 9; requirement that all shelters use an intake/exit model of service; removal of the current Minimum Standards for Shelters and replacement with *Shelter Programs, Operations, and Facilities Standards* as a continued requirement for funding; a requirement that all programs develop "Good Neighbor Agreements" with adjacent property owners (residential and business); and a stipulation that new shelters should not be sited next door to, across the street from, or adjacent to an existing school.

With such attention to the minutiae of program detail, it is difficult to imagine that these recommendations could have been directed with any more specificity at the DIC, which at the time offered shelter services dormitory style (open shelter with "step-up" progress to treatment programs) accommodations, with 250 beds (39 for women, 211 for men), operated transitional housing programs in Census Tract 9; used an intake/exit model of service for women, with plans to develop the same for men; met the standards of the current *Minimum Standards*; and, like all other shelters, had no "Good Neighbor" agreements, but was a participating member of the OTR Community Council and had shared arts programming with the SCPA. And, for 30 years, DIC had been located across the park from the elementary school, soon across the street from the newly sited school.

With peculiar specificity, a citation in the *Report* regarding schools required that

new shelters should not be sited next door to, across the street from, or adjacent to an existing school. Definition of "school" and "adjacent to" must be clearly defined and researched. Further the transition process must address the safety factors in locating new shelters in the future. (Cincinnati/Hamilton County Continuum of Care, Inc., 2009, pp. 1–2)

This extraordinary requirement, codified now by ordinance, can only be interpreted as a step to remove DIC, as the only "siting" question in play was the location of SCPA adjacent to DIC. The requirement of the report to research the definition of "school" included in the prohibition of siting shelters was so disingenuous that it bordered on ludicrous. The *Municipal Code* has defined *school* for decades as follows: "'School' means a facility for educational purposes that offers a general course of study at primary, middle, or high school levels and vocational and trade programs that are incidental to the operation of such school" (§1401-01-S. School). It was blatantly clear that these policies and ensuing implementation steps were directed at removal of the DIC.

Within but a few weeks of the City Council's adoption of the *Implementation Plan*, the board of the DIC was summoned to City Hall for a meeting with the mayor, members of the City Council, staff of CoC, and staff of 3CDC. The DIC board was asked to sign an agreement that the center would be relocated from 12th and Elm Streets, according to plans developed and implemented by 3CDC that included choosing the site, the building, and the best practices model to be used (L. Akers, personal communication, August 24, 2010). The board did not sign the agreement at that time, and negotiations continue.

The priorities of *The Homeless to Homes Report* were clearly and emphatically focused on the urgent need to develop new transitional and permanent supportive housing —the "homes" portion of "homeless to homes." Yet, in an initial implementation maneuver, the CoC issued a request for proposals (RFP) for a new women's shelter of 50 to 60 beds, those beds for single women to be removed from the city's shelter portfolio of 312 beds, purging the entire inventory of shelter beds for women from DIC (39 beds) and Bethany House Services (four beds), as included in the *Consolidated Plan*. Providers of shelter for women were invited to submit RFPs to the CoC for evaluation by a review team of three to five individuals, some from within the state of Ohio and some national homelessness experts. As stated in the CoC RFP, "All members of the review committee will have expertise in the field of homeless services, particularly services to homeless single women, but will be from outside the Cincinnati/Hamilton County area" (Cincinnati/Hamilton County Continuum of Care, Inc., 2010c, p. 4). Shelter providers who might have submitted RFPs were caught off guard by assuming that the selection of an approved provider would also use the CoC model of decision making, which includes review by the Homeless Clearinghouse and the Prince of Peace Process for funding. Instead, planning and selection had been transferred to an ad hoc outside authority, sidestepping and violating deliberative consensus of the community.

Two proposals—one from DIC, the other from the YWCA—were submitted for review by the outside review committee. The award was granted to YWCA (not a provider of shelter for singles under the *Consolidated Plan*), whose proposal contained previously signed letters of agreement between the YWCA and 3CDC and pledges for funding commitments arising from decisions made before the RFP was issued. 3CDC committed to planning, development, and financing to cover a new or renovated building and to "assist in development of facility management, operations and social service standards and procedures" (Cincinnati Center City Development Corporation, 2010b).

The removal of "homelessness from Washington Park" by removal of the DIC is proceeding, with piecemeal dismantling of programs: removal of the women's component, with its public and private funding shifted to the YWCA; relocation of the men's programs facilitated by 3CDC; and requirement for "Good Neighbor" agreements attached to the next funding cycle, where the only potential good neighbors of any sort are those who are intent on removing the Center. This story remains in progress, without considerable community deliberation.

The removal of economic others, particularly those who are homeless, soon took an unusual turn that *did* generate considerable community deliberation. At the same time as the RFP for shelter for single women was awarded to the YWCA, a long-awaited award was made by the Ohio Housing Finance Agency for renovation of the ALI for permanent supportive housing for single women in a funding package of $12.4 million. Although the application of host agency CUB for this tax credit project predated the Homeless to Homes initiative, the ALI plan was included in the report's recommendations and had received the highest score in the most recent round of funding decisions made by the Ohio Housing Finance Agency. As funded in the award, it will bring the capacity of ALI to 152 units in three programs, adding 85 units of permanent supportive housing for single women.

ALI has housed single, vulnerable women for more than a century at its location adjacent to the historic home of Mr. and Mrs. Charles P. Taft, now the Taft Museum of Art. Charles P. Taft was the half-brother of President William Howard Taft; he and his wife gave the land and funded ALI as a gift to the city, placing operation with CUB, the oldest social service agency in the city. It is important to note that residents of ALI became neighbors of the Tafts, no doubt without negotiating a "good neighbor" agreement. Named for the Tafts' daughter Anna Louise Taft Semple, ALI opened in 1909 to house young, single working women who came to the city for employment. It remains operational to date for single women, continuing under the stewardship of CUB. The location of this beautiful, historic building is at Third and Lytle Streets, adjacent to the city's Lytle Park, named after Civil War General William Henry Lytle and watched over by a 12-foot-tall bronze statue of Abraham Lincoln—all at an irresistible location for economic development, as envisioned by locally owned Western & Southern Financial Group.

In January 2011, two weeks after the dedication of Western & Southern's impressive new $320-million skyscraper, the Great American Tower, at Queen City Square, the company and its subsidiary Eagle Realty announced plans to acquire the nearby ALI building and property. Chairman and president John Barrett boldly announced his plans for the acquisition of ALI for "high end condos" to advance the company's plan to "turn Lytle Park into a dynamic gaslight district with dynamite housing, the park in the middle, a new hotel and restaurants" (Bernard-Kuhn, 2011a, p. A1). This stunning announcement brought immediate response from CUB president Stephen MacConnell, reaffirming to the company and the community that ALI is not for sale, nor is it tradeable for other properties, nor is it available to be bought off with $4 million in construction cost savings if relocated, as proposed by Western & Southern. In addition, the CUB board remains committed to going forward with their $12.4 million tax credit project for renovation of ALI. MacConnell also captured the social justice dynamics of this attempted takeover, telling the *Enquirer*, "This is our building. John's [Barrett] sense of entitlement is off the rails a bit, but he's a person I respect and intend to work with as neighbors going forward" (Bernard-Kuhn, 2011a, p. A8).

Unable to make a deal for the purchase of the ALI, Western & Southern turned to the City Council, persuading councilmember Jeff Berding to introduce action to delay authorization of the city's portion ($2.6 million in HOME funds) of the $12.4 million project as unanimously authorized by ordinance (Cincinnati City Council, 2010e) three months earlier. With such action, the funding package would have collapsed, as contract deadlines were imminent and the project could not have proceeded. Berding's probusiness argument for his action was framed as the city's urgent need to increase economic development that would bring additional tax revenue to offset budget deficits. Western & Southern's arguments concerned the authorization of the city funding as unfair and introducing notions disparaging ALI's clientele, now describing them as homeless families, men, and prostitutes. In communication submitted to the Finance Committee, the company wrote,

> Many questions and concerns continue to emerge about the fairness, objectivity and openness of the city's handing of taxpayer-funded low interest loans for the Anna Louise Inn—essentially converting it from its legacy mission as a housing facility for low-income single women to now include a

shelter for the homeless families including males and recovering prostitutes. (Cincinnati City Council, 2011)

In contrast with earlier takeover attempts that had gone unreported, the *Cincinnati Enquirer*, having earlier covered the development plans for the Lytle Park area, reported Berding's City Council item with a front-page, bold headline: "Shelter Plan Hits New Snag, Western & Southern Contests Funding for Anna Louise Inn" (Bernard-Kuhn, 2011b, p. A1). In a curious redundancy, the proposed action before City Council was stated affirmatively to authorize the previously awarded funds for ALI to proceed. Apparently, the company was counting on a majority to vote against their previous ordinance, which had passed 9 to 0. City Council did not reverse course, voting first in the Finance Committee (7 to 1), then a vote in the full Council, where it also passed (8 to 1), to proceed with the funding for ALI.

This maneuver by a major corporation, boldly announcing it was somehow entitled to buy ALI, struck a raw spot in the hearts of the larger community. The *Enquirer*'s electronic blog was flooded with hundreds of messages, at a ratio of 99:1, favoring ALI. Of dozens of letters to the editor published in print editions of the *Enquirer*, almost all support ALI; one (Hebbeler, 2011) captures both the meaning of this current episode and references the earlier losses of affordable housing in the Hope VI renovations of public housing and the soon-to-be-constructed upscale housing at the Banks development:

> Years ago, most of Laurel Homes and all of Lincoln Court were demolished. Those of us who objected to this massive loss of affordable housing were told that mixed-income communities were the way of the future. How is it then that there will be no affordable housing at the Banks and it is desirable to relocate the Anna Louis Inn to make way for more market rate development? What happened to the goals of mixed-income communities? (p. A9)

The second approval of the tax credit project by City Council brought short-lived victory. Denied cancellation of funding for ALI, Western & Southern turned to the Court of Common Pleas (Case No. A1104189) challenging the city's approval of conforming zoning and historic building codes for the project. The court delayed hearing the case until Western & Southern's several appeals to the City Zoning Board of Appeals were exhausted. The day after ALI prevailed with the Board of Appeals, the Common Pleas Court scheduled a hearing some three months hence, at year's end. This schedule was seen by most as timed so the tax credits would expire. Turning for protection under fair housing laws, the women residents of ALI turned to federal court, bringing charges of housing di_ crimination and intimidation against Western & Southern. And CUB has filed for relief from Western & Southern's repeated use of the court system to delay the ALI project until the tax credits expire at year's end.

The plans for the renovations of ALI are proceeding, with CUB firmly holding to its ownership of the building and stewardship of the vision of the Taft family to house single, vulnerable women, for the moment. When the time comes, perhaps Barrett and his Western & Southern subsidiaries will work with CUB to make "good neighborhood" agreements between the company and ALI, as promulgated by the Homeless to Homes Ordinance.

In this unusual episode of policy-driven attempts at removal of economic others, it was the private corporation that turned to public policy for relief from failed market-driven initiatives; it was the nonprofit agency serving economic others, with support from a wider community, that found relief in public policy, for the moment, for one small program serving homeless single women, prostitutes, and economic others.

The impact of privatization of public decision making in the arena of social services and shelter for homeless economic others in these accounts raises alarming concerns about implementation of public social policy. These concerns extend beyond traditional outsourcing human services by purchase of service contracts, operations of information systems for social programs, or even contracting with "experts" to prepare social reports or consolidated plans. By choosing private entities, including those incorporated as public–private partnerships, to manage selected functions of civic enterprise and to execute publicly held responsibilities—in this case, decisions on planning, locating, and funding services for homeless individuals—the city foregoes deliberative process, thereby privileging private authority.

Writing of the constitutional and political implications of privatization, Kennedy and Ritchie (2001) reminded readers that although privatization has champions proclaiming quality, efficiency, and expertise, it places the rule of law in peril:

> While privatization is almost always defended as a method for producing smaller and more responsive government, in fact it simply empowers— *authorizes*—private interests to act under government's imprimatur, shifting the locus but not the magnitude of the task at hand. It privileges authority over the rule of law. (p. 145)

Although the development of *The Homeless to Homes Plan* included some "deliberative process" in the use of a "committee of experts" model to formulate a plan, and the *Plan* was authorized by City Council vote, implementation was privatized by the CoC to actualize the larger goals of 3CDC to develop OTR and "deconcentrate homelessness from Washington Park."

In this avaricious chapter of the city's social and political history, the econocidal, policy-driven steps used to remove homeless economic others from the community expanded beyond direct removal of people or groups to elimination of their services and dismantling their shelters and to overriding proven professional, community-based models of service developed by skilled practitioners. Driven by policy notions of economic homogeneity, this can be compared with a business takeover that undermines stockholders' decision-making authority (bypassing deliberative consensus of the Prince of Peace Process), cheapens product quality for profit (removing shelter beds from communities with great need), and loses consumers who use the product (removing homeless economic others). In the end, by authorizing those without primary interest in the city's responsibilities for the totality of the social–ethical sphere of obligation at all socioeconomic levels, including economic others, and lacking open, accessible provision for recourse for privately made decisions, an entire segment of the community is compromised, along with democratic traditions and principles inherent in the larger community.

Conclusion

I began this study with the story of my social work client Sophie, whose body I was called to identify in the hospital emergency room, where she had been rushed by a life squad from a local SRO hotel. Sophie is gone. So is the last of the city's SRO hotels, recently taken for economic development to be converted to a boutique hotel, financed by public funds for private purposes. Like her counterparts in the collectivity of economic others, Sophie held a precarious place in an entrepreneurial city. This study has revealed that relentless promotion of economic homogeneity in a city with privatized governance nourishes and sustains legalized, sanctioned removal of economic others like Sophie by econocide.

This study documents ways that privatization of city governance, accommodated by enactment of public policies that prioritize and zealously promote economic homogeneity, legitimizes economic inequity. Further, through the privileging of authority over deliberative, democratic processes, social justice for individuals and neighborhoods is jeopardized at all levels of society. When combined, these two dynamics resemble a moral equivalent of genocide in the economic spectrum, camouflaged in the fabric of a market economy and business ideologies, but named "econocide."

Privileging Some

Privatizing functions of city government to public–private partnerships absolves the city of responsibility for the totality of the sphere of public obligation, privileging some sectors of the community over others. In this study, absolution of city government in socioeconomic–political arenas is evidenced in housing policy—planning, zoning, public funding, locating shelters—and in policies for function and use of public space—renovation of public parks, locating schools, freedom of expression in the public square, and exclusion from use. As seen in the accounts in this study, policies like the local Housing Impaction Ordinance, implementation of federal Hope VI, and publicly funded land-banking of buildings for private upscale development are blind to the needs of economic others for economically affordable housing. By design, affordable housing is removed from the market. Similarly, privatizing management of public assets, like management of the public square and authorization for renovation of city parks, restricts access and usage of public space. As a sequel to surrendering governance to private entities in the areas of housing and public space, the city's responsibility for socioeconomic and racial diversity in neighborhoods, and indeed the larger city, is circumvented, especially when not made a contracted requirement of public–private partnership agreements.

Deconcentration as Public Policy

Policy deriving from the notion of deconcentration of poverty, as manifest in Cincinnati, where it was successfully applied to housing policy, poisons public narrative on broader socioeconomic–political dynamics essential to sustaining a humane, inclusive society. It worked to dismantle poor neighborhoods, so it should be used for removing homeless shelters. The first goal was ostensibly to deconcentrate neighborhoods affected by poverty, which soon became deconcentration of poverty, with subsequent proposals to deconcentrate one condition of poverty known as homelessness and social services that ameliorate poverty. At best, meanings attached to deconcentration present an ideological puzzle, and at worst, when applied to the public's business, they can promote socioeconomic chaos. How could it be understood if applied, for instance, to cancer ("deconcentrate cancer"?); would it mean to separate cancer patients from each other or from patients with other diseases, perhaps by diagnostic category? Or remove cancer patients from certain areas of the city? Or perhaps use tools of technology to deconcentrate or break up cancerous tumors? In the instance of "deconcentrate neighborhoods impacted by poverty," does it mean reduce housing density per city block? Or reduce the size of some households so there will be fewer people who are poor per building? Or forbid people who are poor to live on the west or south sides of streets? Or widen the streets to spread housing over larger spaces?

The absurdity of these rhetorical questions on large, complex concepts like cancer and poverty points out the intellectual and moral difficulty in applying the concept of deconcentration to poor neighborhoods, people who are homeless, social services, or conditions like homelessness.

As this study shows, the toxic effects of a city's successful application of "deconcentration," when applied to housing, expanded to policies implemented to remove people who are homeless, result in displacement of certain users of public parks, denial of access to the public square, and restrictions on public speech. And, once used, notions of "deconcentration" became justification for subsequent application as if socially and morally acceptable.

Who Decides?

Who are the "deciders"? When elected officials surrender the responsibilities of government to public–private partnerships, who is authorized to make public decisions? Who is authorized to establish public goals of economic homogeneity that deny socioeconomic–political participation in the community to those who are economically poor, as if that were morally principled? When government surrenders public participation and deliberative processes to closed bodies like the insular boards of public–private partnerships, government is excused from due process of the law and redress of grievances. I believe these questions are broader than matters of mere accountability or contract compliance and that the answers, as experienced in Cincinnati, place democratic principles and deliberative processes at great risk. When policymaking is surrendered to public–private partnerships or privately empowered bodies without accountability to the entire community, and without recourse or provision for redress of grievance, established principles of democratic society are jeopardized and are at risk of being bastardized.

The Market, Seeping Deeply into Social Work

In my decades of experience as a social worker working with people who are poor, often homeless—families, youths, pregnant and parenting teenagers, single men and women—who share both severe economic poverty and poverty-related social and psychological problems, I have observed that they share particular vulnerability to public policies in areas of social welfare, housing, and freedom of mobility and expression. Immediate or long-term remediation of their problems, both personal and systemic, rise and fall on the basis of local, state, and federal public policies that, in my experience, have come to ensure the perpetuation of econocide.

At present, I believe this is attributable to wide acceptance of market-economy business principles that have swept the entire country with the onset of conservative–libertarian political power and have seeped deep into the social policy and social work practice that condone them. Such principles have short-circuited the progressive, socioeconomic–political principles of inclusivity of earlier years and, if perpetuated by social work practice, tarnish our ideals of social justice. They have made it possible, in the name of "best practices," to exclude some while granting others full socioeconomic–political power.

Poverty Knowledge, Policy Knowledge

Sadly, I believe that shifts in public social policy driven by ideologies of the right, as played out in the example of Cincinnati, could not be countered, because our poverty knowledge base is inadequate to meet such ideological challenges. And our policy knowledge is inadequate to safeguard the deliberative processes so essential to our democracy with regard to both substantive policy and social justice. This is particularly troubling for economic others, who are not found in the data sets and information systems that drive current poverty knowledge research, and their absence authenticates business-conceived notions of "best practices." In the case of Cincinnati, it was acceptable to reduce available, affordable housing in the name of removing obsolete public housing projects; similarly, it was acceptable to restrict use of federal entitlement funds for affordable housing by the Housing Impaction Ordinance for the neighborhoods most in need.

Examples are also found at the federal level in the Welfare Reform Act of 1996 and the Quality Housing and Work Responsibility Act of 1998, in which access to public assistance and affordable housing came to be predicated on legislation of personal behaviors deemed undesirable in a conservative political agenda: Prevent teenage pregnancies by promoting abstinence-only campaigns, promote marriage, institute time limits for receipt of economic assistance, and add employment requirements for continued housing assistance, rather than enact economic measures meaningfully related to personal, household, or neighborhood burden of need. In another local example, Cincinnati's Homeless to Homes Ordinance purports to improve services to homeless single people by use of so-called best practices and good neighbor agreements, when in reality it removes shelters for the homeless from certain neighborhoods for purposes of economic development. It also mandates models of service based in business practices rather than human service practices, and it makes First Amendment right to panhandle a criterion for exclusion from shelter.

Without an adequate body of poverty knowledge, the codified intrusion of "best practices" to be implemented by public–private partnerships rather than communities and providers of services solidifies and perpetuates econocide. More alarming, without adequate policy knowledge, principles of inclusion and diversity can be sidestepped as easily as the deliberative processes so essential to democracy.

A Final Word

In the end, it is my hope that this study offers entry into a larger public narrative on economic inequity that challenges many sectors of the community—especially social workers and social researchers, politicians, and the business community—and must include neighborhoods and economic others, no matter how poor or seemingly offensive. Such a narrative could begin to restore deliberative democracy at many levels of decision making—whether in neighborhoods or bodies of elected representatives and whether the concern was housing, social work clients, location of soup kitchens, or economic development projects. Failing to restore decision-making power to include all levels of our public life absolves our city, state, and federal bodies of responsibility for the totality of public obligation and circumvents responsibility for socioeconomic and racial diversity of neighborhoods, of the city or the state.

Econocide is a perfect crime. The crime scene has no body, no weapon, no identifiable perpetrator, no motive but economic homogeneity, and it is littered with policies enacted and sanctioned by elected agents of the public, held harmless by privatization.

References

3CDC—New deal-maker. (2003, July 2). *Cincinnati Enquirer*, p. C6.

Affordable Housing Advocates. (2010a). [Minutes of meeting, April 27, 2010]. Cincinnati: Author.

Affordable Housing Advocates. (2010b). *The state of affordable housing in Hamilton County: The crisis report.* Retrieved from http://www.ahacincy.org/

Alltucker, K. (2000, November 11). Is Over-the-Rhine ripe for development? *Cincinnati Enquirer.* Retrieved from http://www.enquirer.com/editions/2000/11/11/fin_is_over-the-rhine.html

Anglen, R. (2000, June 29). City says no to housing project. *Cincinnati Enquirer*, p. C1.

Anglen, R. (2001, October 9). Housing plan for poor draws fire. *Cincinnati Enquirer*, pp. B1, B5.

Appadurai, A. (2006). *Fear of small numbers: An essay on the geography of anger.* Durham, NC: Duke University Press.

Auletta, K. (1982). *The underclass.* New York: Random House.

Ban low-income rental, middle class flight. (2001, October 11). *Cincinnati Enquirer*, p. B10.

Becker, K. (1995). *Genocide and ethnic cleansing.* Retrieved from http://www.munfw.org/archive/50th/4th1.htm

Benhold, K., & Castle, S. (2010, September 15). France may face legal action over expulsions of Roma. *New York Times.* Retrieved from http://query.nytimes.com/gst/fullpage.html?res=9E02E6D81E3BF936A2575AC0A9669D8B63

Bernard-Kuhn, L. (2009a, September 25). New life for Metropole? 3CDC turns focus to building. *Cincinnati Enquirer*, p. A16.

Bernard-Kuhn, L. (2009b, January 25). A rare chance to remake Over-the-Rhine. *Cincinnati Enquirer*, pp. F1–F6.

Bernard-Kuhn, L. (2009c, January 25). Washington Park: Testing revitalization. *Cincinnati Enquirer*, p. 6.

Bernard-Kuhn, L. (2010, May 15). Shelter gets offer to move. *Cincinnati Enquirer*, p. A1.

Bernard-Kuhn, L. (2011a, January 13). Big plans in works for Lytle Park area. *Cincinnati Enquirer*, pp. A1, A8.

Bernard-Kuhn, L. (2011b, January 22). Shelter plan hits new snag, Western & Southern contests funding for Anna Louise Inn. *Cincinnati Enquirer*, p. A1.

Browne, C. (1985, July). The small hotel proprietor. *Hyde Park Living*, pp. 10–11.

Budzek, M. (2006). [Homeless presentation PowerPoint, MARCC Board, September 8, 2006]. Cincinnati: Author.

Burleigh, M., & Wippermann, W. (1991). *The racial state: Germany, 1933–1945.* Cambridge, England: Cambridge University Press.

Cincinnati Center City Development Corporation. (2004). *Cincinnati Center City Development Corporation progress report July 2003–July 2004.* Retrieved from http://www.3cdc.org/who-we-are/annual-progress-reports/

Cincinnati Center City Development Corporation. (2010a). *Cincinnati Center City Development Corporation progress report year VI 2009.* Retrieved from http://www.3cdc.org/who-we-are/annual-progress-reports/

Cincinnati Center City Development Corporation. (2010b, April 21). *Letter from Stephen G. Leeper, CEO to Charlene Ventura, CEO, YWCA.* Cincinnati: Author.

Cincinnati City Council. (1995a, May 3). *Ordinance No. 155-1995.* Cincinnati: Author.

Cincinnati City Council. (1995b, May 3). *Ordinance No. 156-1995.* Cincinnati: Author.

Cincinnati City Council. (1996a, March 13). *Ordinance No. 074-1996.* Cincinnati: Author.

Cincinnati City Council. (1996b, August 7). *Ordinance No. 229-1996.* Cincinnati: Author.

Cincinnati City Council. (2001, October 31). *Ordinance No. 346-2001.* Cincinnati: Author.

Cincinnati City Council. (2002, December 18). *Ordinance No.398-2002.* Cincinnati: Author.

Cincinnati City Council. (2003a, April 2). *Ordinance No. 084-2003.* Cincinnati: Author.

Cincinnati City Council. (2003b, April 23). *Resolution No. 6771-2003.* Cincinnati: Author.

Cincinnati City Council. (2004a, November 3). *2005–2009 consolidated plan, Vol. I: Profile of Cincinnati.* Cincinnati: Author.

Cincinnati City Council. (2004b, November 3). *2005–2009 consolidated plan, Vol. II: Needs and strategies.* Cincinnati: Author.

Cincinnati City Council. (2004c, November 3). *2005–2009 consolidated Plan, Vol. III: Action plan.* Cincinnati: Author.

Cincinnati City Council. (2005, June 15). *Ordinance No. 218-2005.* Cincinnati: Author.

Cincinnati City Council. (2008a, October 8). *Ordinance No. 347-2008.* Cincinnati: Author.

Cincinnati City Council. (2008b, June 25). *Resolution No. 41-008.* Cincinnati: Author.

Cincinnati City Council. (2009, May 21). *Ordinance No. 129-2009*. Cincinnati: Author.

Cincinnati City Council. (2010a, April 28). *Motion No. 2010-781*. Cincinnati: Author.

Cincinnati City Council. (2010b, June 1). *Motion No. 863-210*. Cincinnati: Author.

Cincinnati City Council. (2010c, March 3). *Ordinance No. 049-2010*. Cincinnati: Author.

Cincinnati City Council. (2010d, November 3). *Ordinance No. 383-2010*. Cincinnati: Author.

Cincinnati City Council. (2010e, November 17). *Ordinance No. 410-2010*. Cincinnati: Author.

Cincinnati City Council. (2011, January 24). *Budget and finance committee agenda item no. 31-201100076*. Cincinnati: Author.

Cincinnati/Hamilton County Continuum of Care, Inc. (2006). *Homeless management information system* [Data file]. Cincinnati: Author.

Cincinnati Hamilton/County Continuum of Care, Inc. (2009). *Homeless to homes: Putting an end to homelessness*. Cincinnati: City of Cincinnati.

Cincinnati/Hamilton County Continuum of Care, Inc. (2010a). *Annual data report: A report on homeless in Cincinnati and Hamilton County, OH* (HMIS 2009 Annual Data). Cincinnati: Author.

Cincinnati/Hamilton County Continuum of Care, Inc. (2010b). *The homeless to homes plan: Implementation report and update*. Cincinnati: Author.

Cincinnati/Hamilton County Continuum of Care, Inc. (2010c). *Request for proposal*. Issue Date June 18, 2010. Cincinnati: Author.

Cincinnati Police Department. (1995). *Arrests for 1992–1994 section 910-13*. Cincinnati: Author.

Cincinnati Police Department. (2004). *Calls for police service and part 1 crimes, January–December, 2003*. Retrieved from http://www.cincinnatioh.gov/police/downloads/police_pdf5188.pdf/

City of Berkeley. (1994). *Municipal code, title 13, chapter 13.37*. Berkeley, CA: Author.

City of Cincinnati. (2003a, July 1). *Center city plan and economic development recommendations move ahead: Lafley to chair new Cincinnati Center City Development Corporation* [Press release]. Cincinnati: Mayor's Office.

City of Cincinnati. (2003b, April 23). *Economic development in the city of Cincinnati, public private partnership: A report of the Economic Development Task Force* (Document No. 2003-6775). Cincinnati: Author.

City of Cincinnati. (2010) *Municipal code City of Cincinnati, OH, codified through ordinance no. 317-2010, effective August 4, 2010*. Cincinnati: Author.

City of Cincinnati Department of City Planning. (2008a, June 9). *Letter to members of social services committee*. Cincinnati: Author.

City of Cincinnati Department of City Planning. (2008b, November 12). *Zoning code text amendments*. Cincinnati: Author.

City of Cincinnati Planning Commission. (1925). *The official city plan of Cincinnati, Ohio, adopted by the City Planning Commission, 1925*. Cincinnati: Author.

City of Cincinnati Planning Commission. (1948). *The Cincinnati metropolitan master plan and the official city plan of the City of Cincinnati*. Cincinnati: Author.

City of Cincinnati Planning Commission. (1980). *The coordinated city plan and the comprehensive land use plan* (2 vols.). Cincinnati: Author.

City of Cincinnati Planning Commission. (2002a). *City planning commission resolution no. 6061-2002.* Cincinnati: Author.

City of Cincinnati Planning Commission. (2002b). *Over-the-Rhine comprehensive plan: A consensus-based plan by people who care.* Retrieved from www.cincinnati-oh.gov/cdap/pages/-3641

City of Cincinnati Plan Review Committee. (1990, December 1). *Report to the City Planning Commission and City Council.* Cincinnati: Author.

Clark et al. v. City of Cincinnati, No. C-A-95-448 (U.S. District W.D. Ohio, 1995).

Clark et al. v. City of Cincinnati, No.1-95-448 (S.D. Ohio, 1998).

Clifford, P. (1995, April 25). DCI's mean-spirited crackdown would be ineffective. *Cincinnati Enquirer*, p. A11.

Cranley, J. (2001a, October 4). *Memorandum to mayor and members of council re: Impaction ordinance.* Cincinnati: Office of Councilmember Cranley.

Cranley, J. (2001b, June 20). *Motion to city council to draft housing impaction ordinance.* Cincinnati: Office of Councilmember Cranley.

Cunningham, B. (2008) [Radio broadcast, April 21, 2008, 2:25 p.m.]. Cincinnati: WLW-AM.

Destexhe, A. (1995). *Rwanda and genocide in the twentieth century.* New York: New York University Press.

D'Intino, E. (2007, December 2). [Letter to the editor]. *Cincinnati Enquirer*, p. D2.

Dohoney, M., Jr. (2008, January 9). *Memo to mayor and members of city council re: Emergency Shelter Grant (ESG) allocations and details on shelter house volunteer group (d.b.a. Drop Inn Center) allocations* (Document No. 2008-0025). Cincinnati: Office of City Manager.

Dohoney, M., Jr. (2010, February 18). *Memo to mayor and members of council re: Ordinance—Metropole funding agreement.* Cincinnati: Office of City Manager, Inter-departmental Correspondence.

Dow, D. (2007, October 9). Fountain Square snub riles Bearcat fans. *Cincinnati Enquirer*, p. A1.

Drescher, S. (1977). *Econocide: British slavery in the era of abolition.* Pittsburgh: University of Pittsburgh Press.

Econometrica, Inc., & Abt Associates, Inc. (2006, January). *Multifamily properties: Opting in, opting out and remaining affordable.* Retrieved from http://www.huduser.org/Publications/pdf/opting_in.pdf

Eggleston, Greater Cincinnati Coalition for the Homeless, Grace Place Catholic Worker House v. City of Cincinnati, No. 1:10CV395 (U.S. District Court for Southern Ohio, 2010).

Euclid, Ohio v. Ambler Realty Co., 272 U.S. 365 (1926).

Fairbanks, R. B. (1988). *Making better citizens: Housing reform and the community development strategy in Cincinnati, 1890–1960.* Urbana: University of Illinois Press.

Fair Housing Act, P.L. 88-352, 42 Stat. § 3601-3631 (1968).

Fein, H. (2007). *Human rights and wrongs: Slavery, terror, genocide.* Boulder, CO: Paradigm.

Flannery, G. (1997, November 29). Who's park is it? *CityBeat,* p. 4.

Fonseca, I. (1995). *Bury me standing: The Gypsies and their journey.* New York: Vintage Books.

Fraser, A. (1992). *The Gypsies.* London: Blackwell.

Fraser, J., & Nelson, M. H. (2008). Can mixed-income housing ameliorate concentrated poverty? The significance of a geographically informed sense of community. *Geography Compass, 2,* 2127–2144.

Gans, H. J. (1990). The dangers of the underclass: Its harmfulness as a planning concept. In *People, plans, and policies: essays on poverty, racism, and other national urban problems* (pp. 328–343). New York: Columbia University/Press Russell Sage Foundation.

Gerckens, L. C. (1980). Glancing back. *Planning, 46,* 23–26.

Gerckens, L. C. (2001). The comprehensive plan in the 20th century. *American Planning Association 2001 National Planning Conference.* Retrieved from http://design.asu.edu/apa/proceedings01/GERCKENS/gerckens.htm

Gilder, G. (1981). *Wealth and poverty.* New York: Basic Books.

Gillespie, E., & Schellhas, B. (Eds.). (1994). *Contract with America: The bold plan by Rep. Newt Gingrich, Rep. Dick Armey and the House Republicans to change the nation.* New York: Times Books.

Goetz, E. G. (2000). The politics of poverty deconcentrations and housing demolition. *Journal of Urban Affairs, 22,* 157–173.

Goetz, E. G. (2003). *Clearing the way: deconcentrating the poor in urban America.* Washington, DC: Urban Institute Press.

Goetz, E. G. (2004, November/December). The reality of deconcentration. *Shelterforce*(138). Retrieved from http://www.shelterforce.com/online/issues/138/deconcentration.html

Goodman, R. (2008, March 27). Ralph C. Browne owned downtown hotels. *Cincinnati Enquirer,* p. B5.

Good plan for Washington Park. (2004, June 12). *Cincinnati Enquirer,* p. B14.

Greater Cincinnati Coalition for the Homeless. (2001). *Homelessness in Cincinnati, OH: A study of the causes and conditions of homelessness prepared for the Greater Cincinnati Coalition for the Homeless by AIR, Inc., September, 2001.* Retrieved from http://homehttp://homeless.cincy.com/pages/content/reports.htmlless.cincy.com/pages/content/reports.html

Greater Cincinnati Coalition for the Homeless et al. v. City of Cincinnati et al. U.S. Dist. Court, Case. No. 1:08-CV-00603-HJW-TSB. 2008. 2010.

Green, R. (1995, January 12). Proposal gives boot to beggars. *Cincinnati Enquirer,* p. A1.

Hammelrath, M. (2006, February 7). *Letter to mayor Mark Mallory and all council members.* Cincinnati: Over-the-Rhine Foundation.

Harrington, M. (1962). *The other America: Poverty in the United States.* New York: Macmillan.

Hauck, J. W. (2004, October 4). *Letter to Urban Design Review Board re: 3CDC plan to renovate Fountain Square* (Document No. 2004-99034). Cincinnati: Urban Design Review Board.

Hebbeler, K. (2011, January 18). Subsidized housing lost. *Cincinnati Enquirer*, p. A9.

Heimlich, P. (1995, May 12–18). Spare change and short fuses. *Everybody's News*, p. 7.

Horn, D. (2010, August 18). Metropole plan challenged. *Cincinnati Enquirer*. Retrieved from http://www.cincy.com/

Housing and Community Development Act of 1974, P.L. 93-383, 88 Stat. 633 (1974).

Housing in Over-the-Rhine. (2000, June 30). *Cincinnati Post*, p. 16A.

In re: Cincinnati policing (Collaborative Agreement), No. C-1-99-317, US District Court, Southern District of Ohio, Western Division (2001).

Italy: Census of Gypsies begins. (2008, July 19). *New York Times*, p. A6.

Jargowsky, P. A. (2003). *Stunning progress, hidden problems: The dramatic decline of concentrated poverty in the 1990s*. Retrieved from http://www.brookings.edu/~/media/Files/rc/reports/2003/05demographics_jargowsky/jargowskypoverty.pdf

Johnson, K. (2002, July 8). Crime keeps Cincinnati reeling. *USA Today*. Retrieved from http://www.usatoday.com/news/nation/2002/07/08/usat-cincinnati.htm

Kennedy, S. S., & Ritchie, I. (2001). *To market, to market: Reinventing Indianapolis*. Lanham, MD: University Press of America.

Knack, R. E. (1980). Where planning counts: In Cincinnati, planning is considered a virtue. *Planning, 46*(10), 14–19.

Korte, G. (2002a, December 13). City's planning director resigning amid breakup. *Cincinnati Enquirer*, p. 14.

Korte, G. (2002b, November 29). Mayor puts pressure on shelter. *Cincinnati Enquirer*, p. B1.

Krantz, C. (2010, June 7) Panhandlers in spotlight again, *Cincinnati Enquirer*, p. B1

Krueckeberg, D. A. (Ed.). (1994). *The American planner: Biographies and recollections* (2nd ed.). Piscataway, NJ: Center for Urban Policy Research/Rutgers University.

Leaders chart way to oppose Section 8. (2009, February 24). *Cincinnati Enquirer*, p. B1.

Leibovitz, J., & Salmon, S. (1999). 20/20 vision? Interurban competition, crisis and the politics of downtown development in Cincinnati, OH. *Space & Polity, 3*, 233–255.

Lemkin, R. (1944). *Axis rule in occupied Europe: Laws of occupation analysis of government, proposals for redress*. Washington, DC: Carnegie Endowment for International Peace.

Lewis, O. (1959). *Five families: Mexican case studies in the culture of poverty*. New York: Basic Books.

Lewy, G. (2000). *The Nazi persecution of the Gypsies*. New York: Oxford University Press.

Local Initiatives Support Corporation. (2009). *Hope VI: Cincinnati, Ohio*. Retrieved from http://www.lisc.org/content/publications/detail/936

Marglit, G. (2002). *Germany and its Gypsies: A post-Auschwitz ordeal*. Madison: University of Wisconsin Press.

Margolick, D. (1992, December 18). Klan's plan for cross stokes anger in Cincinnati. *New York Times*. Retrieved from http://www.nytimes.com/1992/12/18/news/klan-s-plan-for-cross-stokes-anger-in-cincinnati.html

McCarty, C. (2005, October 12). *"CityLink Center"—Bank street development chef club* (Document No. 2005-10626). Cincinnati: Cincinnati City Council.

McNeil, J. R. (2006, October 31). *Memo RE: Request for legal opinion: 42 U.S.C. §200c ("Religious Land Use and Institutionalized Persons Act" or "RLUIPA").* Cincinnati: Interdepartmental Correspondence Office of City Solicitor.

Metropolitan Area Religious Coalition of Cincinnati. (2005, May 27). *Executive Board minutes, May 27, 2005.* Cincinnati: Author.

Moller, W. E., & Moertl, P. (2001, October 23). *Memo to mayor and members of city council re: Questions and administrative review regarding the Ordinance to Reduce the Concentration of Poverty.* Cincinnati: City Interdepartmental Correspondence.

Monk, D. (2001, October 12). Over-the-Rhine's future is now. *Business Courier of Cincinnati.* Retrieved from http://cincinnati.bizjournals.com/cincinnati/stories/2001/10/15/story1

Monk, D. (2003, January 3). Razing the roof: Some laud developer for his action, while others simply bristle. *Business Courier of Cincinnati.* Retrieved from http://www.bizjournals.com/cincinnati/stories/2003/01/06/story4.html

Moynihan, D. P. (1965). *The negro family: The case for national action.* Washington, DC: U.S. Department of Labor.

Myrdal, G. (1963). *Challenge to affluence.* New York: Pantheon Books.

Neubeck, K. J., & Cazenave, N. A. (2001). *Welfare racism: Playing the race card against America's poor.* New York: Routledge.

O'Connor, A. (2001). *Poverty knowledge: Social science, social policy, and the poor in twentieth-century U.S. history.* Princeton, NJ: Princeton University Press.

Ohio Revised Code Chapter XVII, Sec 1710.01 (Special Improvement district) (2000).

Osborne, K. (2000a, June 29). Council deadlock kills funding for Over-the-Rhine housing plan. *Cincinnati Post,* p. 15A.

Osborne, K. (2000b, July 1). Tarbell: Let's redevelop Vine St. *Cincinnati Post,* p. 10A.

Peale, C., & Alltucker, K. (2001, August 19). Land shifts for a landlord. *Cincinnati Enquirer.* Retrieved from http://www.enquirer.com/editions/2001/08/19/fin_land_shifts_for.html

Personal Responsibility and Work Opportunity Reconciliation Act of 1996, P.L. No. 104-193, 110 Stat. 2105 (1996).

Phillips, D. C. (1995, April 25). Begging the question: Downtown's future depends on stopping panhandling. *Cincinnati Enquirer,* p. A11.

Plan to fix Washington Park good for children, neighbors. (2007, December 2). [Letter to the Editor]. *Cincinnati Enquirer,* p. D2.

Popkin, S. J., Katz, B., Cunningham, M. K., Brown, K. D., Gustafson, J., & Turner, M. A. (2004). *A decade of HOPE VI: Research findings and policy challenges.* Retrieved from http://www.urban.org/url.cfm?ID=411002

Pushing out panhandlers: Street beggars are driving away shoppers and businesses. (1995, January 13). *Cincinnati Post,* p. 13A.

Quadagno, J. (1994). *The color of welfare: How racism undermined the war on poverty.* New York: Oxford University Press.

Quality Housing and Work Responsibility Act of 1998, P.L. No.105-276, 112 Stat. 2518 (1998).

Rager, D. (2006, August 2). *Memo to mayor and members of city council: Revision to CMC section 713 permits for Fountain Square.* Cincinnati, OH: Office of the City Manager.

Religious Land Use and Institutional Persons Act of 2000, P. L. 106-274, 42 U.S.C. § 2000cc (2000).

Residents fed up with Section 8. (2009, August 20). *Cincinnati Enquirer,* p. B1.

Riordan, T. H. (2002, January 30). *Memo to mayor and members of council re: Vine street community project & ReSTOC contract* (Document No. 2002-4617). Cincinnati, OH: Cincinnati City Council.

Rose, M. M. (2006, March 26). A quiet rebirth in Over-the-Rhine. *Cincinnati Enquirer,* p. A1.

Rose, R. (2008). *Europe's largest minority Roma and Sinti demand equal rights.* Retrieved from http://www.un.org/Pubs/chronicle/2006/webArticles/120106_rose.htm

Rosenthal, E. (2008, May 16). Italy arrests hundreds of immigrants. *New York Times,* p. A6.

Rosin, H. (2008, July/August). American murder mystery. *Atlantic, 302,* 40–54.

Rotundo, R. (2010, June 30). Let neighbors keep their Washington Park [Letter to Editor]. *Cincinnati Enquirer.* [Posted in electronic edition, June 30, 2010, 5:24 p.m.]

Roulette v. City of Seattle, 850 F. Supp. 1442, W.D. Wash. (1994).

Save pool, OTR residents say. (2007, November 29). *Cincinnati Post,* p. 9.

Shirey, J. (1996, February 28). *Memo to mayor and members of city council re: Privatization of Fountain Square management.* Cincinnati: Interdepartmental Correspondence.

Social Security Act of 1935, P.L. No. 74-271, 49 Stat. 620 (1935).

State v. Burnett, 93 Ohio St.3d 419, 2001-Ohio-15810 (2001).

Stewart B. McKinney Act of 1987, P.L. 100-77, 42 U.S.C. 119, §11302 (1987).

Stradling, D. (2003) *Cincinnati, OH: From river city to highway metropolis.* Charleston, SC: Arcadia.

Taking Back Our Streets Act of 1995, H.R. 3, US House of Representatives (1995).

Tina Deal, a minor, by Frank L. Deal, her father, et al., Plaintiffs v. The Cincinnati Board of Education et al., No. 402 US 962, 91 S. Ct. 1630, 29 L. Ed. 2nd 128 (District Court, 1965, US Supreme Court, 1971).

U.S. Census Bureau. (1952). *Census tract statistics, Cincinnati, Ohio and adjacent areas, 1950 population census report* (Vol. 111, Chapter 11). Washington, DC: U.S. Government Printing Office.

U.S. Census Bureau. (2000). *Census 2000 summary file 1 100 percent data.* Retrieved from http://factfinder.census.gov/servlet/DatasetMainPageServlet?_program=DEC&_lang=en

U.S. Department of Housing and Urban Development. (2009). *Definitions of eligibility.* Retrieved from http://www.hud.gov/offices/cpd/affordablehousing/training/web/calculator/definitions/part5.cfm

United States Housing Act of 1937, P.L. No. 75-412, 50 Stat. 888 (1937).

Wachsmann, N. (2001). From indefinite confinement to extermination: "Habitual criminals" in the Third Reich. In Gellately, R., & Stoltzfus, N. (Eds.), *Social outsiders in Nazi Germany* (pp. 165–191). Princeton, NJ: Princeton University Press.

Wiers, B. H. (2007). *Stable integrated communities*. Cincinnati: Cincinnatus Association.

Wilson, W. J. (1980). *The declining significance of race: Blacks and changing American institutions*. Chicago: University of Chicago Press.

Wilson, W. J. (1987) *The truly disadvantaged: The inner city, the underclass, and public policy*. Chicago: University of Chicago Press.

Works Progress Administration. (1987). *Cincinnati, OH: A guide to the queen city and its neighborhoods*. Cincinnati: Cincinnati Historical Society. (Original work published 1943)

Wuerstle, M. (2009). *Regulating social service facilities: A study of alternatives for Cincinnati, Ohio's neighborhoods*. Unpublished master's thesis, University of Cincinnati.

Zeleznik, M. (2010, February 11) [Transcript of radio interview on Impact Cincinnati with S. Leeper and B. Donabedian, WVXU-FM]. Retrieved from http://www.wvxu.org/impact/impact_archiveview.asp?ID=2/11/2010

Index